BECOMING

ME

BECOMING
ME

by

Kristi S. Smith

authorHOUSE®

AuthorHouse™
1663 Liberty Drive
Bloomington, IN 47403
www.authorhouse.com
Phone: 1-800-839-8640

Published by AuthorHouse   03/26/2012

ISBN: 978-1-4685-7402-9 (sc)
ISBN: 978-1-4685-7403-6 (e)

Library of Congress Control Number: 2012905616

DEDICATION

SHANE, THIS BOOK is for you. I might often joke about being married to my horses, but you are the most important relationship in my life. Thank you so much for always believing in me and supporting my crazy dreams. I love you.

FORWARD BY LINDA PARELLI

I REMEMBER THE first day I met Kristi and her horse Maxi, they were my demo subjects on one of our tour stops. I remember Maxi was quite young, a pretty paint mare with a very strong opinion! Being an introverted horse, with a dominant nature, she had found the way to do less and make Kristi do more. Showing Kristi how to use more psychology, the results came quickly. I was impressed by her capacity to learn and make changes, and when she said she had decided her goal was now to become a Parelli Professional, I was not surprised . . . and quite hopeful. A lot of people who make this statement don't usually have what it takes to see it all the way through, mentally, emotionally, or physically.

In this book Kristi shares what it took for her to achieve her dream, and on the way become one of the most outstanding instructors on our team. She also plays a highly inspirational role showing the depth and quality of the relationship and impressive achievements with that same horse, Maxi.

One of my own mentors, Glynn Braddy, once said "Personal developments are rarely comfortable or convenient". Doing what it takes to achieve your dream is not for the fainthearted, and perhaps the only quality you really need is to never, ever, ever give up. Kristi takes us all along on her own journey, feeling what she's feeling and time and again coming to admire that very quality in her — she just doesn't give up. There were many moments where she could have quit. And she didn't. I think it's so inspiring and educational to take that walk in her shoes.

This book is a raw and honest account of one woman's dedication and commitment to a dream. I love how she entwines life lessons with horsemanship, and shows how the horses have this way of holding up a mirror to us. Kristi kept looking in that mirror, whether she liked it or not. She shows us how learning to be more natural with horses helps us all grow in ways we never imagined. Kristi is and continues to be one of my favorite people to be around. She's the consummate student and what she can now share with others is what makes her a powerful teacher and mentor in her own right.

CHAPTER 1

Making Up My Rules

How OLD WERE you in your earliest childhood memory? Have you considered how that memory has shaped your life? I was around 4 years old in mine. My little brother, Dan and I were playing outside in the yard. It was a warm and sunny summer's day and we were playing tag. This was one of our favorite games because the tag included tackling each other to the ground. We were having fun playing, laughing and rolling around in the green grass even though we were trying to hide from the frightful scene that we could hear emanating from inside the house. Our mom and dad had been screaming at each other all day and we were just trying to stay out of the way. This was a normal day in our house and Dan and I knew we were better off making ourselves scarce. We were giggling and chasing each other around the yard when all of a sudden our mother burst from from the front door yelling to us to start running! My dad came bursting out right after her with his hunting rifle in hand. He was crazed with anger. We all instantly went into panic mode. He yelled at me and Dan to get back in the house. Mom scooped us up and started running down the street. The plan was to go to my aunt's house a few blocks away. Dad was yelling at us to get back inside. His rage increased when we did not turn around. Our panic intensified when he began to fire shots over our heads. I never believed that he would actually shoot any of us. But still, we ran for our lives. It was difficult to keep up with my mom. She was nearly dragging me by the hand. I lost my footing and nearly fell several times. She would lift me up by the hand and I would be airborne for a few strides before my feet would touch down again.

I remember that day so vividly because that was the first day I made rule about my life. I decided that I would never allow a man or anyone else to ever treat me that way. I was terrified but also humiliated. I remember thinking we were only making things worse by running and it would be better if we just stayed. We would have to go back there eventually anyway. I know that it may be hard to believe after a story like that, but I was a daddy's girl. I knew he loved me and didn't want to hurt me or my brother. But in that moment, I didn't see my daddy. The man who was shooting at us was a monster. I knew that when I was old enough to choose for myself I would only choose men who would treat me with dignity and respect. I decided I would learn to take care of myself so that I was never put in a position to feel so vulnerable again. To this day, I am hypersensitive to any hint of domestic violence. I cannot even bear to watch it in a movie. I instantly go back to that day and relive the terror and shame that my loved ones and I went through. That day I developed an extreme need to feel in control of my environment. It also caused me to develop a deep sense of self reliance. I needed to feel safe and there was no one but me to provide that. I would spend the next twenty-five years trying to prove how tough and independent I was. This choice helped me to become an over achiever, but it prevented me from understanding and appreciating the intimacy and even power that can come from being vulnerable. I started to build a wall and would continue to do so for many years to come.

That day my dad was shouting at me specifically, not my brother, to get back to him while my mother pulled on my hand to keep me running with her. I know it sounds strange, but ultimately, I felt a deep sense of loyalty to him and I felt a great deal of betrayal for running away and disobeying his order to get back in the house.

My father was a terrible husband. He was never faithful and often physically abusive to his wives. He was not good at holding a job or taking responsibility for the well being of and providing for his family. But, to his kids he was a great dad. He played with us and took a great deal of interest in our upbringing. He often bragged to his friends about how tough and special I was. He made me feel important and loved. I knew that his anger and violence were not directed at me or Dan. It never was. It was always directed at our mother.

I was not really afraid on that warm summer's day, until I heard him fire the rifle. The pop of the shots scared me to death. I wanted to go back to him, but I knew that my mother was not going to let go of me. I felt out of control and I made a decision that day to never allow anyone to put me in a position where I couldn't choose for myself again. My obsession with control and independence was driven very deep on that day. Even at such a young age, I began to seek out opportunities to take control and be my own person. As a kindergartener I would insist on walking myself the six blocks to school. By the time I was in the first grade, I could set my own alarm and get myself ready for school on time with little or no adult supervision. I think about the children I know today and would never consider leaving a six year old at home alone to fend for herself. It seems ridiculous and like child neglect to me today. But, at six years old, I was certain that I could take care of myself and I often did.

Most of my childhood was very miserable and full of domestic violence. My father was verbally and physically abusive to all of his wives and mistresses. He was married at least three times. I have memories of several other woman who he never married. He was an alcoholic and also abused recreational drugs. His temper was never directed at me in a physical way and he is not a villainous character in my memories or my life. I know that many of you reading this story will think that it is weird for me to speak so highly of my dad after what I have just told you. But, I have come to understand that it is possible to love a person without liking or approving of their actions. Life was hard for all of us. We were all doing the best we knew how. I have always loved my father dearly. He just did not possess the tools that were required for him to live the life he wanted. He was frustrated and disempowered and he didn't know how to do anything differently. Those who hurt others are generally feeling hurt themselves. Some of the things he did to his wives were truly horrific and I carried the scars of his actions for nearly twenty years. I was almost proud of those scars, but they came at the cost of my mental and emotional health. I have come to accept that his actions had nothing to do with me and it is not necessary for me to explain or justify anything that he did. My relationship with my dad is up to me, and that is all that I can be responsible for, *my* relationships. I can love the man even if I didn't understand or approve of his conduct. He gave me the gift of self confidence and although I was 30 years old before I could appreciate that, I cannot thank him enough. I have forgiven him for his actions and come to peace with my feelings of love and devotion for him. I will explain more about how and why I did that later.

Learning The Truth

When I was five years old the woman that I had called mom my whole life told me that she wasn't my "real" mother. My biological mother had not been in my life since I was six months old. I had no memory of her. But, somehow, I always knew that there was something different about Dan's relationship with his mother versus my relationship with her. I did not feel the same way about her that he did. She looked at him differently than how she looked at me. She was great and did a great job raising me as her own. I never felt as though she did not want me in her family, but I knew that something was not being said between us.

One day, while Dan and I were playing in the living room of our sparsely furnished home we began to argue about where babies come from. I said that babies come from their mommies' tummies. Dan replied that I did not come from his mother's tummy. We got into a fairly heated argument about it and started yelling at each other. We finally caught my step mother's attention from the kitchen. She felt that she had better explain to me what Dan was trying to say. She sat down on the couch and drew me close to her. I was standing between her legs and my arms hung over her knees. She started telling me about my "real" mother. She explained that my father had been married to another woman before her and that they had a baby together. I was that baby. But, when I was six months old my parents had their marriage annulled and my father was granted custody of me. She did not explain why my mother disappeared from my life at that point. I later discovered that my dad had been cheating on my biological mom with Dan's mother, and my mom found them in bed together. This single event caused me to grow up without knowing what it is like to have both parents in the same place at the same time. They despise each other to this day. I guess that I come by my ability to hold a grudge quite naturally. Theirs has lasted over thirty-seven years. I now choose to not allow that kind of poison into my daily consciousness. Their inability to forgive and move on has cost them numerous moments of joy and that is a price that I am not willing to pay. There is no wrong so deep that I am willing to live my life with such pollution in my heart.

Standing there looking up at my step mother, Kathy in our living room, I could tell that she was worried about how I might feel about this news. Kathy had accepted me as her child and never made me feel like I did not belong. She was a sweet, kind and caring woman, and as she told me the story of my birth and parents, for some reason, I was not surprised. It was something that I had always felt. I could tell that she was ready to hold me and console me. I wondered if I was suppose to be upset. I didn't know what to feel, so essentially, I tried to feel nothing. It didn't matter, I thought. It doesn't change anything. I am a daddy's girl anyway. I don't need a mother. It was at this point I began to reject any sort of femininity. I wanted nothing to do with acting like a girl or being girly. To this day, I do not like to wear pink and feel uncomfortable admitting to any kind of feminine need or desire. I decided on that day that being feminine meant being weak and I was going to show everyone how strong I could be. I began to live the role of tomboy. I liked that title. I was proud to be a tomboy. I wanted to be stronger, faster and smarter than all the boys because if I could do that, then I could prove to everyone that I didn't need a mother and that it didn't matter that mine was not present in my life. I didn't need to feel any pain because it didn't matter. I was too tough for that kind of girly neediness and vulnerability. I was growing my impenetrable skin and hardened heart.

Becoming a Step Sister

When I was eight my dad was moving on to his third wife. Being committed to one woman would prove to be a life-long struggle for my father. I would make this transition with my dad while my brother stayed with his mom. I was very close to my brother and we were both very affected by this separation. I felt as though I was losing the one person who knew what I was going through. I am sure that my brother was feeling abandoned by his father and maybe even by me. My heart was sick. I still long for the strength of bond that we had prior to that life change.

My father's new wife had five kids: four boys, one girl, and now one step daughter. Their father had been killed a few years earlier in a car accident. They were still grieving his loss and did not care to invite another man and his daughter into their lives. My life proceeded to get worse than ever before. I was never welcomed into that family. No one really wanted me there, especially my new step sister, Vicky. She had become very accustomed to her life as the only girl, and I was not an appreciated part of her daily life. Vicky took every opportunity to remind me that I did not belong or fit in to her family. It was during this time that I began to despise the term "step" in relation to family relationships. All that meant to me at the time was, this is a person who was not invited into my life and I don't want her here. I had no allies. My father was busy being a newlywed. My brother was living with his mother, and I felt very alone. There were many nights that I would cry myself to sleep and pray to God to please allow me to not wake up in the morning. *No one would even notice*, I thought. I am thankful for that unanswered prayer.

I find it nearly impossible to recall any happy memories from this timeframe in my life. I don't really know why, but it seemed that my father was never around. I was constantly left alone with these children who made no attempts to hide their discontent with my presence. It seemed no matter how hard I tried to be a good member of this family, I was never really accepted. I would try to do chores without being asked and would then be told that I did them wrong or not good enough. I couldn't hide away in my room because I shared it with my step-sister. The only place that I felt successful was in school and sports. I excelled at both. Even then, my step-mother would knock me down by saying that I might be book smart, but that I had no common sense. I still bear the emotional scars of those words. I am very sensitive to any type of insult that may be about my intelligence. I work at not reacting to those type of comments, but they will still evoke a strong emotional response in my core.

To make matters worse, my dad insisted that I start calling this woman mom. It did not feel good to me. It did not feel good to her. And it enraged her children. But, like I said, I was a daddy's girl and endured it all to please him. I would never dream of disobeying him. Making him proud of me was the only source of joy I had at that time.

Whiskey: My First Great Teacher

I was very fortunate to attend a small country school from kindergarten through sixth grade. My class sizes averaged around ten students. My teachers were from an era when people became teachers of children because they were passionate about teaching. I give these people a great deal of credit for my confidence as a learner and my personal successes to this day. They instilled in me a belief that I could be anything I wanted as long as I was willing to do the work. I loved school. It became an escape for me. That would be a pattern that would last throughout my life. I would participate in as many extracurricular activities as possible. I was in the band. I loved being in school plays. I was a member of several clubs. I played every sport that girls were allowed to play. I would do anything to not have to go home at the end of the day.

Around the time I inherited four brothers and a sister, I started spending time at an aunt's house. My aunt Peggy had horses! I had been out to ride her horses frequently throughout my life. She lived five miles out of town on a country road. Around the age of nine I started riding my bike there as often as I could to ride. There was something about these animals that I was drawn to. With them I felt like I belonged. I finally had a family who wanted me. I was happy and felt whole whenever I was with them. Not all of my cousins wanted me there, but once I was on a horse, it didn't matter. I had 3 avenues for escape. One was school, the second was sports, and the third was Aunt Peggy's horses. I became obsessed with all three.

Aunt Peggy had a mare that was my favorite at the time. Her name was Whiskey. She was a big beautiful sorrel quarter horse. I mostly remember how powerful I felt when I rode her. She gave me the ability to run faster, jump higher, and be more than what I could be with my feet on the ground. I loved riding her and was more than happy to take the long bike ride for the opportunity to spend the day with her. She would be the first friend I would have that made me feel as though I was "home".

Horseless

When I was in fourth grade, my dad moved us to Texas for a year. My step-mother had family there. Their marriage was filled with the same challenges that I had seen with my brother's mother. I think that my dad and step-mother were looking for a fresh start. It was during my time in Texas that I began to feel uncomfortable with the tomboy image. My step-mother was a hairstylist and had cut my hair very short. Between my hair cut and style of dress and general mannerisms, it became a little difficult to tell whether I was a little boy or a little girl. I wanted to be perceived as strong—not as a boy. The culture in Texas was unlike anything I had ever experienced. I had never been in an environment where being a girly girl was so coveted. The whole southern bell phenomenon made me extremely uncomfortable and took away my ability to feel safe and special in school. I lost all of my escapes. I didn't want to play sports because that would fuel the flame of me being gender-confused. I was teased constantly in school because of how I looked. Aunt Peggy and my horse family lived hundreds of miles away. It was a very dark time in my life. I was miserable and my shell grew harder. I am glad that this period only lasted for one year. I am not sure that I would have been able to survive much longer than that.

A Sense of Belonging: Mel

When I was twelve, my father was leaving his third wife and going back to his second. I was happy to leave Texas, but I just didn't want to move back in with the previous wife. I knew that wasn't going to be a scenario that would last. I wanted to stay in one place and feel as though I had some stability in my life. I knew that the only way I was going to get to do anything differently was if I came up with an alternate plan for myself. The only place that I had experienced anything that made me feel good was with the horses at my Aunt Peggy's house. She had taken in a few of my cousins for various reasons, so I knew that she was open to looking after everyone else's kids. I decided to ask my dad if I could go live with her. He said that I could, but that I had to be the one to ask her. I called her that day to tell her my situation and what I wanted to do. She talked it over with her family and by the following afternoon I was moving in with them. It was the first time I felt a true sense of empowerment and the ability to control my destiny. I quickly became addicted to that feeling. It would later prove to be a great imbalance in my life that I would struggle to overcome.

I will always be eternally grateful to my aunt Peggy and her family. They gave me a place to belong when I was feeling lost and I didn't have anywhere else to go. I was not the only extra in the household and taking me in was a bit of a burden for this family. Aunt Peggy did the best that she could and I love her unconditionally.

This environment was also polluted with domestic violence. My uncle was an intense man without a lot of patience. My memories of him are either really really great or really really awful. We had great times riding four wheelers and horses, going camping, and hanging out with family friends. However, my uncle had a very short temper and I also remember him doing things like punching my eleven-year-old cousin with a closed fist in the face out of frustration with his need for constant attention. He was abusive to my aunt and their kids. I remember there being lots of screaming and crying. Watching someone get hit was a regular thing. I did my best to avoid this by learning how to become invisible. I did not want to jeopardize my place here because no matter how difficult life was, I still had horses here. So, I would disappear as often as I could, either into some type of after school activity or with a horse.

I had one cousin who took every opportunity to make my life miserable. She would incessantly tease and insult me. She would tell me that I was ugly and that no one wanted me there. But, I could hide from her and everyone else with the HORSES!! I didn't feel as though I had the love and acceptance of my very own family, but I had horses in my life. I was willing to put up with any and all abuse from the humans in exchange for the opportunity to be with the horses. Shortly after I moved in I got to pick one out of the herd that would be mine! His name was Mel and he would become my greatest childhood friend.

Mel was a dun quarter horse and when he came into my life he was only two years old. He spent thirty days with a trainer and then became my partner. I spent every possible moment with him, before school, after school, weekends, and all summer. All I wanted to do was ride. He was kind of spooky and sometimes hard to catch. I can honestly say that during my years with Aunt Peggy, I spent more hours with that horse than any single human being. With him I felt special and wanted. I felt as though I had someone who I could depend on and share happy moments with. Mel seemed to feel differently about me than anyone else. He seemed to be more at ease when I was the one going to catch him. There were days that I would be with him from morning until night. He was my escape in to a world that made me feel happy and loved. We lived in a very rural community. Our nearest neighbor was at least two miles down the road. Our road was not heavily traveled. We also lived near an abandoned railroad track. I could ride for about three miles down the road and then loop back on the railroad track. Mel and I would spend entire days making this loop. We would gallop across any open field, stop to pick the wild raspberries or just sit under a tree and enjoy each other's company. Occasionally one of my cousins would come with us, but most of the time it was just me and Mel. He passed away unexpectedly in 2006 when he was hit by lightning. I miss him to this day. He was a ray of sunshine in a very dark period of my life.

Some of my happiest childhood memories are of camping and trail riding with my family. Aunt Peggy and the rest of us would load up the horses and go camping for long weekends. We would go swimming, hiking, fishing and most importantly trail riding. There were days that I would literally spend all day with Mel. I would only get down when I was forced to take a break for a meal and or at the end of the day to go to bed. I loved those trips and to this day work to recapture the joy I felt on those trails and in those woods. I am so grateful to my aunt and her family for those memories. This family instilled in me a deep sense of accountability and a very strong work ethic. They have been and continue to be a very important part of my life.

Meeting My Mother and Pete

At the age of thirteen a new challenge came my way. I had a great-aunt on my biological mother's side of the family who would periodically spend time with me. She was the only member of that side of the family to make an effort to see me in those days. One day she called me to ask if I would like to attend my great-grandmother's birthday party. She had never taken me to see the rest of the family before. I knew that it would be an opportunity to connect with a family that I did not know. Although I was scared, I was desperate to make that connection. I had some idea that my mother, whom I had no memory, might be there. She was not, but nearly all of her siblings were as well as their mother, my maternal grandmother. I had a nice time with everyone and was sure to share my contact information with anyone who wanted it. My grandmother passed that information along to my mom.

A few weeks later, I received a letter with a return address and name that I did not recognize. I asked Aunt Peggy about it and she suggested that it might be my mom. Eeeek! I hadn't even considered that! My heart started pounding! What did she want? I had never really considered that she would ever be a part of my life. She was never talked about. I had just accepted my life as the invisible outsider in my aunt's home. Now, here she was—my mother—trying to make contact with me at a time in a young girl's life that is already confusing and emotional.

Needless to say, puberty was not much fun for me. Not only was I an awkward pre-teen and young teenager, but I also had such a difficult time trying to understand my life and who I was meant to be in it.

I read the letter with a pounding heart and sweaty palms. She made no apologies and gave no explanation for her absence in my life and still hasn't. She merely asked me to give her a chance to be my mother. I had no reason to say no. I had never really had someone express such a desire to be with me. I was wanted! I did not have bad feelings towards her. I had never been given much explanation about why she was not present in my life up to that point. I couldn't really process what I was supposed to feel. She was my chance at getting to know what it feels like to live in a home where I was not considered a burden or charity case. I had never had a mother before and I was at an age where I desperately wanted one. So we made plans to spend that Easter together.

On Easter we agreed to meet on neutral ground at my grandmother's home. It was all very awkward and overwhelming. Not only had my mother been absent, but so had her whole family. I met the entire family that weekend. I knew none of these people. The weirdest part was that everyone pretended like this was something we did all the time, like I had been visiting on Easter for the last thirteen years. The crazy thing was that I had some memory of this place. Still,

I do not really understand how or why. There are pictures of me at my grandmother's as a toddler, but as I said, I have no real memory of my mother until I met her at thirteen. It is my understanding that there were short periods of time when my mother tried to participate in my life. And for unknown reasons, it never worked out.

My mother has four sisters and they all grew up barrel racing. There were HORSES at my grandmother's house! Two of my aunts even went to the National High School Finals Rodeo to run barrels! I was so very excited to be a part of this family! My grandfather was also a bull rider. There was an entire room full of trophies, buckles and ribbons on display to emphasize my family's passion for horses and rodeo. It was very exhilarating. I was eager to know more. I started to feel as though I might actually fit in here. Maybe I would get to a place where I didn't feel like an outsider. Maybe I could belong.

My mother and I spent a couple of days getting to know each other. We did the normal Easter activities. I had cousins who were much younger than me so we had an Easter Egg hunt and exchanged candy filled baskets. I got to groom and pet the horses. My aunts recalled stories of being on the road and the adventures they had running barrels all over the Midwest. It was a good first meeting. I felt hopeful.

After that first encounter, my mother and I continued to exchange letters and phone calls. We got to know each other little-by-little. Then, summer break came and she invited me to spend the entire summer with her. My Aunt Peggy wanted me to discuss this plan with my dad before committing to it. It was the first time in my life I remember my dad telling me no. Something happened to me as an infant that I believe my father blames my mom for. I don't know what it is. The two of them have kept that a secret. So I told my father that unless he could give me a good reason not to, I was going to spend the summer with my mom. He continued to dance around the reasons why I shouldn't. So, without a good reason not to, I went to my mother's. My dad was so upset by my decision that he did not speak to me for several years after that. In my heart, I felt like my mother had abandoned me as an infant, and then so did my father when I was thirteen. My protective shell grew thicker and harder. These events are what I believe instilled in me a belief that the only person I can count on is me. I abandoned any thought of relying on anyone but myself. I had to look out for number one, right? If I didn't, who would?

That summer at my mom's was awkward, but it still felt pretty good to have a family of my own. We got along pretty well and she had HORSES!! Not only did she have horses, but she had the next big love of my life, Pete. Pete was a big powerful chestnut gelding with one blue eye and one brown. He was an outstanding horse and an incredible athlete. Whenever I felt like life had gotten out of control, I would tell Pete about it, and he would make me feel better. I missed my friend Mel very much, but Pete was doing a great job filling in. My mom started teaching me about barrel racing and we competed at some local shows. I really wanted to call myself a barrel racer, but we mostly just dabbled in the sport that summer.

Making Things Permanent

As the summer drew to a close and I was preparing to return to Iowa when my mother asked me to consider living with her full-time in Missouri. She quite literally begged me. She still hadn't apologized or offered any explanation for her absence in my life, but somehow I still felt that I owed it to her to at least give her a chance. Had it been just her and I, we probably would have been good together. However, there was another player in this game—her husband. To say that this man was unstable would not even come close to giving you a clear picture of him. His mood swings were wider than the Grand Canyon. Some days we were a happy family full of laughter and joy. Other days would find me and my mom racing down the street on foot to the police station to seek protection and shelter from his violence. To make matters worse, I was estranged from my father because of my desire to know my mother. And, even though I had explained how traumatizing it was for me to call my step-mothers "mom" at my dad's request, my mother asked me to call this man dad. Every time I called him that, I felt disgusted. It was extremely painful to me that my dad had excused himself from my life, and my mother's husband was not the kind of guy to inspire any kind of healing. It was a very confusing and painful time in my life.

An evening spent running from my step-dad and having both parents in a knock-down-drag-out fight caused me to decide that spending some time away would be good for me. I wanted to go and spend some time with my Aunt Peggy. My thought was that I would recharge my batteries, get a fresh perspective and then be ready to recommit to being with my mother. However, the trip "home" for me only made me want to stay in Iowa. I explained to Aunt Peggy how things were going with my mom and her husband. Through painful tears, I asked if I could please come home. She and my uncle agreed that I could and the wheels were set in motion.

The next hurdle was going to be telling my mother. I did not want to hurt her. I did my best to let her know that I still loved her, but that I just couldn't live in that environment any more. On the phone she sounded understanding and compassionate. Those feelings would soon be overshadowed by her hurtful actions during my transition back to Iowa with my aunt. When we met for me to collect my belongings, she kept everything that she had ever given me, including a stuffed toy that she gave me as an infant. She kept school clothes and school supplies along with anything else she felt might hurt me the way that I had hurt her. Needless to say, it took some time for those wounds to heal, on both sides. We would not speak to each other for many months. I began to understand that all I had to do to cause someone to remove themselves from my life was to do something that upset them. My shell grew harder still, and I developed the belief that there is no such thing as unconditional love.

I was thirty years old before I could appreciate the many gifts that my mother has given me. I know that my ability to take a difficult situation and turn it into something positive comes from her. I get my resourcefulness and strong will from her. She is an amazing woman and my love for her grows every day. I choose to love her not in spite of her short comings, but because of them. She is a remarkable woman and I wouldn't trade her for anything. I am lucky to have had a set of life experiences (mostly with horses) that have allowed me to let go of the ugly part of my past and embrace the gifts that those events have given me. I know that many people go to their grave never gaining that perspective and peace. I believe those kinds of unattractive thoughts are the cause of some cancers. It is just a theory I have that motivates me to let go of the ugliness.

Acting My Age

From the age of sixteen until thirty I carried a huge chip on my shoulder. I'd gotten a raw deal and someone was going to pay for it. I didn't have anyone in particular in mind, but the world owed me! I spent a lot of time and energy trying to prove to people that I was tough and didn't need anyone. The only person I could count on was me. If I wanted something, it was up to me to make it happen. There are some good things about having this kind of attitude. I am very self reliant and motivated. I accomplished a great deal based on my own desire to excel. I refused to fall into that broken home, underprivileged, pathetic category. I did not need a lot of poking and prodding to go above and beyond. I was not about to make any excuses that would justify failure, even though no none would have blamed me. I was committed to success and achievement. I was determined to live above my genealogy and upbringing. I did achieve beyond what was expected of me and that makes me feel important and special. However, this is not a great attitude if one wants to live a life full of the joy of relationships, collaboration, and contribution. This attitude did develop in me a high level of determination and responsibility for myself. I was very accomplished through high school and into college. I graduated with honors and was selected by my student body and teachers to give a speech at graduation. I excelled at most of the things I set my mind to through sheer will and determination. I was a cheerleader. I sat first chair in the concert and jazz bands. I had artwork that won state awards. I graduated 10th in my class with a 3.85 GPA. Ultimately, I attended a private college for two years funded by scholarships for music, foreign language, and academics. My attitude was not openly harmful. Most people would consider my life a success story at this point. However, I was very lonely and unfulfilled. I was harboring a great deal of resentment and hostility and my anger was consuming me.

CHAPTER 2

Discovering My Passion

AFTER HIGH SCHOOL graduation I spent two years at a private college studying Spanish. I wanted to teach English as a second language. My main reason for this choice was that Spanish class in high school was easy. I seemed to have a knack for picking up foreign languages. The only way I could think of turning that skill into a career was to become a teacher.

The private college I attended was located in the middle of what I would describe as a city. As a small-town, farm-raised Iowa girl, I consider anything over ten thousand people a thriving metropolis. I grew up in a town with a population of less than seven hundred. I was really outside of my comfort zone and did not feel a part of the community at college. Most of my peers were attending college on their parents' dollar and they spent a great deal of their time partying and redecorating their dorm rooms. I was on three scholarships along with the maximum amount of federal aid available to me. I even had to have myself declared as an independent student so that I could increase the amount of money I was eligible for. I was on my own as far as funding my education was concerned, so I found ways to make it happen. It would have been a great deal easier for me to attend a state school. However, I made up my mind on that private college and there was no stopping me—mostly because I was told that I wouldn't be able to do it. I stuck it out for two years just to prove that I could, even though less than six months in I knew that I was on the wrong path.

During that time, I was dating a boy who was attending the local community college. We were hanging out at his apartment one afternoon and I noticed the booklet that listed all of the available courses at that college sitting on a table. I began thumbing through it just out of curiosity. When suddenly I came to a section titled "Horse Science." I had no idea such a program existed! I was instantly excited and interested in learning more. I had always wanted to have a career in horses, but I felt like there was no way to make that happen. I had asked my high school guidance counselor, but he did not have any good advice. I grew up in the Midwest. Most people owned horses for recreation mostly. There aren't a lot of performance opportunities or examples of people earning a living in the horse industry. You might as well say that you want to be a famous artist or to star on Broadway. I had discovered the pathway to my dreams, and in some ways it was. I began to make arrangements to transfer that day.

Pheobe

I learned a great deal during my time in the Horse Science program. I took courses on genetics, first aid, even grooming and general facility development and maintenance. But, the most important courses to me were those on training horses. I was exposed to all of the big name clinicians and horse training methods at the time, but the most important exposure was to the Parelli Natural Horsemanship program. I was not an easy sell at first. I wanted to get to the fancy stuff. I wanted to look like an expert. I couldn't see the value in the fundamentals that the Parelli program is based on. My interest was peaked when the program was presented to me as a means for colt starting. Because I could not find a way to become a performance horse trainer, I had decided to become a professional colt starter and the Parelli program was presenting me with a step by step process for doing that. It seemed easy enough. Later, three trips to the emergency room would help me to realize that the colt starting process is a lot more involved than a+b=c. It would be many years before I would appreciate this process as an art form in and of itself.

A great horse came into my life during my college days with a lot of lessons to teach me. Her name was Phoebe. She was a chestnut registered morgan and when we met she was just two years old. She had been donated to the college and soon became my project. She was nearly wild and completely undeveloped as a riding horse. I was her partner for a full year. I put the first rides on her using the knowledge I had gained from my studies. She was an extremely willing partner and the process went smoothly. She was the first horse I ever rode bareback and bridle-less and she sparked in me an extreme desire to learn more about the Parelli Natural Horsemanship program. I have a tattoo of her likeness on my left shoulder. She went on to be one of the most reliable mounts in the college's herd of lesson horses. She ignited in me a belief that I could make it as a professional horse trainer.

Bud

Another college project horse would have a very different influence. Phoebe was my second project horse, my first project horse was a nine-year-old, gorgeous dark bay mustang named Bud. He'd been captured in Nevada at the age of seven. At the time of our pairing he'd only been gelded for two weeks and was still affected by the effects of testosterone. His owner was forthcoming about this horse's tendencies. He told me the horse was a complete gentleman on the ground. But, riding was another story. All attempts at riding this horse had ended in disaster and more than one person had been hurt. I accepted him as a project on the guidance of my instructors. I trusted their judgment and felt that I would not have been encouraged to take this horse if I wasn't ready for him. Knowing what I know now, that decision seems ridiculous and irresponsible. I would soon find out just how deeply troubled this horse was and just how determined he was to not be ridden.

I spent several weeks with him on the ground trying to prepare him to be ridden. He was a skeptical young man and it didn't take much for him to lose his confidence. Any change in routine and he would explode. I tried very hard to prepare this horse for our first ride. I used every technique that I'd been given from dozens of different programs. Finally, one day, I decided I had run out of things to do with him on the ground and was ready to try riding him. I prepared him on the ground, got him saddled, and then asked my instructor for advice on how to proceed. I told her what I had done and that I thought he might be ready to ride. Her response was "You'll never know unless you try." Those words would have a profound impact on my ability to trust someone to guide me on my horsemanship journey for years to come.

With that, I proceeded to fork a leg over my little mustang's back. I know now that I should never have gotten on. If I were to get on a horse today feeling what I felt that day, I would immediately get off. As I swung my leg over, I caused the saddle to slip sideways a little bit. As soon as I put my butt in the saddle, I knew that this horse was not okay with me being up there. He was a giant ball of tension and so was I. I wanted the saddle to be centered if anything were to go wrong, so I grabbed the saddle horn and gave it a yank to put the saddle back in the middle of Bud's back. With that motion, my little mustang came unglued and my world literally turned upside down! To this day, that was the most extreme horse incident I have ever experienced. This horse flung me so violently, and I flew high enough in the air that he had enough time to kick me in my lower back on the way down. I was 21 years old. This was the first time I realized I was a mortal human being, that riding horses was dangerous, and that I could be killed. I was a bit of a daredevil as a kid. But, this experience changed all of that. I found my fear, and it wasn't of dying. I was afraid of living and getting hurt bad. That fear lingers to this day, although the Parelli Program has helped me to lessen it and I continue to chip away at it every day.

When I hit the ground, I also lost consciousness for a few seconds. When I came to, my instructor was at my side and telling me to hold still. I had the wind knocked out of me and was pretty disoriented for several minutes. I was feeling ready to shake it off by the time the school nurse showed up, but she, of course, would not let me get up. I had trauma to my lower back and was told to remain still until the ambulance arrived. Did she just say ambulance!?!? I had never seen the inside of an ambulance before, and to make matters worse, that day was freshman orientation day. The arena was full of shiny, new, young hopefuls looking to see what life at the big college was going to be like. I doubt that they expected to see an array of emergency vehicles and a student hauled away on a stretcher.

When the paramedics arrived I was duct taped to a back board and hauled off to the emergency room. At the hospital, my doctor talked to me about internal bleeding and bruised organs. This conversation further deepened my new fears. Ultimately, this experience would leave me with more emotional scars than physical ones. I became afraid of colt starting and somehow a fear of jumping horses attached itself as well. I had never been afraid of either before, but this fear is something that I continue to chip away at to this day. In recent years I have made huge progress on both, but I will tell you more about that later.

This would not be my only accident in college that required a trip to the emergency room. Over those two years, I would end up with several concussions, bruises, and what I believe was probably a fractured forearm. I was too poor to go to the doctor, so I just put my arm in a sling that I bought at the drug store until it didn't hurt anymore. I endured dozens of injuries, yet I was considered one of the more promising students in my class. I was awarded the "Outstanding Student Award" during my second year. None of that would translate into the ability to earn a living doing something I thought I would love to do.

Showing Rosie

I did get a small taste of life earning a living as a horse trainer. While I was in college, I worked on a small paint horse farm. This farm primarily raised western pleasure horses, and I was hired to clean stalls and feed horses. I cleaned around thirty stalls twice a day and fed a herd of about fifty to feed in the morning and at night.

Because I did not have any experience with pleasure horses, it took me a long time to convince the owners to give me a chance to do anything with any them other than feed them and clean up after them. I finally talked the owners into letting me take on one of their mares that was having trouble getting pregnant as a project at school.

Her name was Rosie. She was a large red roan overo paint mare and she was a beautiful sweet soul. We moved her into the college's barn, and I began learning about pleasure horses. I would eventually take and show her successfully at the collegiate level. Unfortunately, that success would be the beginning of the end of my relationship with the paint horse farm. The work I had done with this particular mare had caused the owners to take interest in her as a performance horse instead of the baby maker they's intended her to be. Due to my lack of experience, I could not show her for them professionally, so they took her from me and gave her to their daughter to start showing. I was left without a project horse for school and this decision could have affected my grade for class. My feelings were hurt and I would eventually have to quit working for the farm. Chapter 3: Forever Partnerships

My Human Partner: Shane

The most important life-changing relationship in my life began while I was in college. I met my future husband. I was a typical college student in that I wanted to have a good time while I was creating my future. I was taking a full class load as well as working and living at the paint horse breeding farm. Most days I had around two hours of chores to do before my first class started at 7:30 am and another two hours of chores after my last class ended around 5:30. But, somehow, there was always energy left to go out and have a good time.

My favorite way to blow off steam was to go out dancing. A friend and I would go to a local dance club every Thursday and Saturday night. Thursday nights were Rock and Roll nights, and Saturday night the DJ played country music. We used to say that Thursdays were for short skirts and Saturdays were for our tight jeans and cowboy hats. We were young, fit extroverts and enjoyed being outrageous and drawing attention to ourselves. It would be on one of these outings that I would meet Shane. Our favorite bar was a roller skating rink before it was a dance club and had a huge dance floor. Our favorite place to be was at the back of the bar. There were two shoe-shine chairs that sat well above everything else. As soon as we arrived, we'd try to position ourselves in those chairs so that we could see and be seen. I felt as though we were perched on our thrones to be waited upon by our loyal subjects.

One Saturday night we both zeroed in on a guy who was playing pool with a bunch of others. He was the best looking guy in the bar. He was wearing a cowboy hat and tan blazer. I remember thinking that he was probably a jerk because he was so gorgeous. No guy could look that good and be a nice guy too. I am very happy to say that I was terribly wrong. I spent the entire night making google eyes at him and trying to get his attention. He never noticed me. It would be several weeks before he would utter the first words he ever said to me, "Would you like to dance?" It was worth the wait, and I was over the moon! Our relationship began with an intense physical attraction and would soon grow into something much more. Shane has been the most important ingredient in my journey, and I am so thankful for his support and influence.

Our relationship progressed very quickly. I was still trying to prove to everyone how powerful and in control I was. On the night Shane finally asked me to dance, I had declared to my girlfriend that I was going to make him mine. I was dressed to kill in a tiny little skirt and was much more outrageous and obvious with my advances than usual. Our relationship was very passionate from the beginning, but what was surprising was how sensitive and supportive Shane was. When we first started dating, I was still working at the paint horse farm. Shane would often offer to come and help me do the chores. I wanted to marry this guy right away!

Over the next few years, our relationship would progress with that same intensity and fire. Within months we were living together and in less than a year we were making plans to buy property and build a house in the country so we could have horses and so that I could have a horse training facility of my own. The step of marriage, however, would come much more slowly. I am Shane's second wife and he was not going to jump into another marriage without feeling as sure as he possibly could that this one was going to work out. He also has two daughters that he needed to protect from further pain and disappointment. There were times when I felt as though it might never happen for us, but I am very happy that we stuck it out and continue to thank the gods for bringing this man into my life. To this day, I have never met a man with such integrity, loyalty, and lovability as Shane. It is common to meet people who are passionate about animals who loose touch with humans. There is no relationship more important to me than my marriage. Shane is the single greatest thing that has ever happened to me.

Everything Means Something

Becoming a step-mother would prove to be one of the most difficult things I would ever attempt to do. In the beginning, I felt as though my childhood had prepared me to be a great step-mom. After all I had been a step kid and remembered well how I would have liked my step parents to be. And for the first several years, things went pretty well between Shane's girls and I. We had ups and downs, but I felt good about my relationship with them. They have a really great mother and she was very supportive of my role in their lives.

The oldest and I clicked because she felt like a little mini me. She loved horses and was excited to go and do horsey things with me. I was still working at the paint horse farm when we first met and she loved going to do chores with me. From the ages of eight to twelve she thought I was cool. The youngest daughter was a bit more girly, but she liked me because her dad liked me, and we got along just fine.

It wasn't until they became teenagers that I really came to appreciate how great my Aunt Peggy was when I was a teen. The most frustrating part of being a step-parent is only being able to offer an opinion. All I get to do is say how I would handle things, and then I am just meant to stay out of the way. Although the girls' mother has always made me feel included. I have learned a great lesson that I cannot control all aspects of my life and that my reality is not everyone's reality. I care very deeply about my step-daughters and want nothing but success for them. They have taught me to let go of the illusion of control. They are their own people and they need to go through their own ups and downs to figure out what kind of life works for them. I really want to protect them from harm and pain, but just like horses, I cannot offer them any advice unless they have asked me for it. The only difference between horses and my step-daughters is that with horses, I know how to cause them to ask my advice. People are more complicated. Imagine all of the confrontations that could be avoided if we only offered advice when we were asked for it. This is particularly difficult with children, but still a good policy. The trick is to cause them to willingly ask you for your advice. I must admit that I continue to struggle with that one. My step-daughters have taught me more about being a great horseman than they will ever know.

The Death of a Dream

I never officially graduated the Horse Science program. I find it ironic that I am sitting here writing a book when I am one Composition credit shy of an Associate's degree. However, I did not feel as though having that piece of paper to hang on my wall was going to make or break my career as a colt starter. In 1997, I made the decision to quit school and hang my shingle out as a local horse trainer.

I had a friend who owned a boarding facility. We worked out a business deal. I could use his facility to grow my business. He collected the money for board on my client's horses and I charged a separate fee for training. I tried for five years to create a successful business as a colt starter. During that time, I had the privilege of starting about ten colts a year. Most of these horses were pretty straight forward and easy to get under saddle. However, there were a handful I really wasn't prepared for and my time with them increased my fears that began with the little mustang in college. Two more trips to the emergency room caused me to realize that my dream had turned into my nightmare. I started to dread going to the barn every day. I would make excuses and soon started asking the barn owner for his his help with my training horses. He would eventually take over the training business and I decided that I would get a "real" job and only keep my personal horses for recreation. My dream died.

It was extremely painful, and I recall feeling a sense of surrender to a life that was not going to be filled with passion, but with a daily drudgery of doing whatever it takes to pay the bills. A piece of my heart shriveled. I would go through several jobs trying to find one that didn't make me miserable. I worked as a fork lift operator in a factory for around 18 months. I delivered the mail and even worked as a school bus driver. Each day at any one of these jobs was torture. I knew that I had so much more to offer the world than just an eight-hour shift. I wanted to make a difference and feel as though I had something unique and special to bring to the table. All I needed to do those jobs was to be able to fog a mirror. I refer to those as the dark years. I believe that you can only fully appreciate the light when you have experienced some of the dark. I am very motivated to never go back to just doing what it takes to pay the bills. Because of the pain and discontent I felt during those years, I am committed to filling each day with my passion. I work each day to be great at what I do so that I can live a life of fulfillment and joy, and not just getting by.

My Prince Charming: Rocky

One of the first gifts given to me by my husband was a horse. We had been dating for about a year and I was about to "graduate" from college. I did not have a horse of my own and I was desperate for one. Shane agreed to help me. I was looking for a two year old that hadn't been started under saddle yet. I was about to become a professional colt starter and I felt as though I needed to start one of my own so that I could use that horse as advertisement for my business. I wanted something athletic and dramatic looking. I searched for several weeks before I found just what I was looking for.

He was a two-year-old leopard Appaloosa. I fell in love with him the moment we met. The day I met Rocky, he was in a pasture with two other young horses. When I went to meet him, the woman who sold him to me gave a whistle and all three horses came galloping to the gate. The other two horses were fairly plain and did nothing dramatic on their way to see us, but Rocky was proud and majestic. He raced to us with his head high and tail in the air. As he reached us, he pranced, snorted, and showed off. My heart raced and I knew instantly that I had found the partner I was looking for. He would become my prince charming.

Rocky was boarded at the same facility where I had tried to grow a horse training business. The day I moved him to our friends' barn was the day he earned the name Rocky. We turned him out in a paddock by himself so that he could get used to his environment before introducing him to any of the other horses. He immediately began striking and squealing at one of the more dominant horses across a gate. The barn owner and I began were concerned that one or both of the horses would end up with a leg tangled in the gate and in a terrible wreck. We decided to open the gate and just let them sort out their dominance issues. That was when the two really started to have it out. They were fighting just like the wild mustang stallions I had seen on National Geographic videos. They reared up at each other and knelt down to bite at each other's knees. Both looking for the other to yield and therefor claim the role of herd leader. I was terrified that Rocky was going to get hurt. The other gelding was a great deal bigger and was already the herd leader. Rocky didn't back down. All we could do was stand back and let them sort things out. By the time they finished, they were great friends and mutually grooming each other. The older gelding won that battle, but Rocky had earned the right to be in his herd.

Getting Rocky under saddle using the methods explained by Parelli Natural Horsemanship went pretty smoothly. We bonded very quickly and I spent every spare moment with him. I rode him successfully for over a year until the day fate would change everything forever. I had arrived at the barn in the early afternoon just as I had done hundreds of times before. The barn owner's wife is my good friend and I intended to visit with her before I played with Rocky. As

I got out of the car, I looked for him. He was standing near the fence and nickered to me. Nothing looked out of place so I called out to say hello and told him I would be out to play with him soon. I went inside and visited with my friend for around thirty minutes. When I went back outside Rocky had not moved. I remember thinking that was unusual.

I went to him with the intention of bringing him in and getting him ready for a ride. But, as I got close I saw one of the most horrific sights I had ever seen in my life. The fence that Rocky was behind was something that is called high tensile wire. It is a steel wire pulled very tight. Rocky's hind leg was woven between the many strands of wire and his flesh was hanging from the bone. I could literally see the large bone in his lower leg and the groves that the wire had put in it. Rocky must have lied down near the fence and got his leg through. Then, he probably got up and felt panicked by being trapped in the fence. Horses are naturally claustrophobic because their natural defense is flight. He pulled hard enough to break the 6 inch wooden corner post that was about thirty yards away from where he was. He was standing calmly now and looking to me for assistance. I had a moment where I wanted to panic and loose my mind, but I gathered my thoughts and raced to the house for help. The barn owner got the horse trailer ready for the trip the horse hospital while my friend and I cut Rocky out of the fence with wire cutters.

He loaded onto the small trailer like a champion and we raced to the hospital. The prognosis was pretty grim. The wire had completely severed the tendon that Rocky used to move his hoof as well as punctured a joint sack in a major joint. What all of that meant was that Rocky was not likely to ever be 100% sound again. I was devastated. My whole life revolved around this horse. The next decision I had to make was did I want to spend the thousands of dollars and months that it would take to heal his wounds with no guarantee that he would ever get back to a quality of life that was humane? Or did I want to end his suffering? It was an impossible choice, but I could not bear the thought of not at least giving him a chance to try and heal. So, I made a commitment to him. I would keep trying as long as he kept trying.

Rocky spent six more weeks in the hospital on IV antibiotics and complete stall rest. I visited him every day. After that, he would come home, but have to remain on complete stall rest for another six months. We needed him to move as little as possible. I had to change his bandages every day during that time. Horses are designed by nature to move up to ten miles a day. Most horses forced to do that much stall rest would develop a type of mental illness that horse trainers call vices. Horses will do things like weave back and forth the way an orphan baby does when he doesn't get held enough. They will paw at the walls or become agitated. Rocky never did any of that. He was patient and calm, always. He would often lie down in his stall to rest. I would go and lie with him and just cry over the lost potential. I felt such guilt for not protecting him and keeping him safe. My heart was broken.

It would take eighteen months before Rocky would be well enough to be ridden again. He actually got to a spot where I thought he was going to be okay. I was riding him again and learning a great deal from him. Then, about two and a half years after his accident, he started to show signs of lameness in the opposite hind leg. The vet diagnosed him with degenerative arthritis and informed me that he was never going to be 100% or even 80% again. I still feel sad when I think of how great we could have been together. My relationship with this horse was easy and natural. We truly enjoyed each other's company and he will forever hold a special place in my heart. He is now helping a friend of mine with her riding confidence. He is now her prince charming. Everything happens for a reason. If Rocky had never gotten hurt, I would have never met my next great teacher.

My Savior: Maxi

It took several weeks, but I came to accept Rocky was not going to be the partner I needed for my business. I love him unconditionally and was devoted to him no matter what. But, I began to look for a new horse that would be athletic enough to help me achieve my goals. Shane and I had our own place and we were boarding a few horses for friends. One of those friends had just purchased a black and white paint yearling. He was gorgeous, playful, outgoing, and he was going to be HUGE! I fell in love with him instantly. I was disappointed to find out that his human was not interested in selling him to me, so I called her horse's breeder to inquire about the next year's foal crop.

I told the breeder of my attraction to the young gelding and asked her if she had bred that gelding's mother back to the same stallion. She informed me that she had and so I placed an order. I told her that I wanted a filly (a female) and that she must be black and white. I wanted her to have a similar personality to her brother. And lastly she needed to have enough white to qualify for regular paint horse papers. If you don't have enough white, the horse gets registered as a solid paint. Solid paint papers generally means that the horse is less valuable. But I didn't want her to have so much white it would be overpowering.

The following spring, the breeder called me to inform me that my horse had been born the night before. I immediately rushed to the farm to meet her. She was everything that I had asked for and more. She and her mother were in a foaling stall. Maxi was just twelve hours old. I anxiously peaked my head over the half wall inside the dilapidated barn to see her and fell in love instantly. She marched boldly over to me as if to say, "Who are you, and what do you want?" I knew from that moment that she was meant to be with me and that we would do great things together. I made arrangements to buy her that day. She had to stay with her mom for the first 5 months of her life, but she has been my girl from the moment we met. I would visit her at the breeding farm several times a week. And was over the moon the day I finally got to bring her home. She instantly made herself at home with my herd and she has been with me ever since.

My Human Partner: Shane

THE MOST IMPORTANT life-changing relationship in my life began while I was in college. I met my future husband. I was a typical college student in that I wanted to have a good time while I was creating my future. I was taking a full class load as well as working and living at the paint horse breeding farm. Most days I had around two hours of chores to do before my first class started at 7:30 am and another two hours of chores after my last class ended around 5:30. But, somehow, there was always energy left to go out and have a good time.

My favorite way to blow off steam was to go out dancing. A friend and I would go to a local dance club every Thursday and Saturday night. Thursday nights were Rock and Roll nights, and Saturday night the DJ played country music. We used to say that Thursdays were for short skirts and Saturdays were for our tight jeans and cowboy hats. We were young, fit extroverts and enjoyed being outrageous and drawing attention to ourselves. It would be on one of these outings that I would meet Shane. Our favorite bar was a roller skating rink before it was a dance club and had a huge dance floor. Our favorite place to be was at the back of the bar. There were two shoe-shine chairs that sat well above everything else. As soon as we arrived, we'd try to position ourselves in those chairs so that we could see and be seen. I felt as though we were perched on our thrones to be waited upon by our loyal subjects.

One Saturday night we both zeroed in on a guy who was playing pool with a bunch of others. He was the best looking guy in the bar. He was wearing a cowboy hat and tan blazer. I remember thinking that he was probably a jerk because he was so gorgeous. No guy could look that good and be a nice guy too. I am very happy to say that I was terribly wrong. I spent the entire night making google eyes at him and trying to get his attention. He never noticed me. It would be several weeks before he would utter the first words he ever said to me, "Would you like to dance?" It was worth the wait, and I was over the moon! Our relationship began with an intense physical attraction and would soon grow into something much more. Shane has been the most important ingredient in my journey, and I am so thankful for his support and influence.

Our relationship progressed very quickly. I was still trying to prove to everyone how powerful and in control I was. On the night Shane finally asked me to dance, I had declared to my girlfriend that I was going to make him mine. I was dressed to kill in a tiny little skirt and was much more outrageous and obvious with my advances than usual. Our relationship was very passionate from the beginning, but what was surprising was how sensitive and supportive Shane was. When we first started dating, I was still working at the paint horse farm. Shane would often offer to come and help me do the chores. I wanted to marry this guy right away!

Over the next few years, our relationship would progress with that same intensity and fire. Within months we were living together and in less than a year we were making plans to buy property and build a house in the country so we could have horses and so that I could have a horse training facility of my own. The step of marriage, however, would come much more slowly. I am Shane's second wife and he was not going to jump into another marriage without feeling as sure as he possibly could that this one was going to work out. He also has two daughters that he needed to protect from further pain and disappointment. There were times when I felt as though it might never happen for us, but I am very happy that we stuck it out and continue to thank the gods for bringing this man into my life. To this day, I have never met a man with such integrity, loyalty, and lovability as Shane. It is common to meet people who are passionate about animals who loose touch with humans. There is no relationship more important to me than my marriage. Shane is the single greatest thing that has ever happened to me.

Everything Means Something

Becoming a step-mother would prove to be one of the most difficult things I would ever attempt to do. In the beginning, I felt as though my childhood had prepared me to be a great step-mom. After all I had been a step kid and remembered well how I would have liked my step parents to be. And for the first several years, things went pretty well between Shane's girls and I. We had ups and downs, but I felt good about my relationship with them. They have a really great mother and she was very supportive of my role in their lives. The oldest and I clicked because she felt like a little mini me. She loved horses and was excited to go and do horsey things with me. I was still working at the paint horse farm when we first met and she loved going to do chores with me. From the ages of eight to twelve she thought I was cool. The youngest daughter was a bit more girly, but she liked me because her dad liked me, and we got along just fine.

It wasn't until they became teenagers that I really came to appreciate how great my Aunt Peggy was when I was a teen. The most frustrating part of being a step-parent is only being able to offer an opinion. All I get to do is say how I would handle things, and then I am just meant to stay out of the way. Although the girls' mother has always made me feel included. I have learned a great lesson that I cannot control all aspects of my life and that my reality is not everyone's reality. I care very deeply about my step-daughters and want nothing but success for them. They have taught me to let go of the illusion of control. They are their own people and they need to go through their own ups and downs to figure out what kind of life works for them. I really want to protect them from harm and pain, but just like horses, I cannot offer them any advice unless they have asked me for it. The only difference between horses and my step-daughters is that with horses, I know how to cause them to ask my advice. People are more complicated. Imagine all of the confrontations that could be avoided if we only offered advice when we were asked for it. This is particularly difficult with children, but still a good policy. The trick is to cause them to willingly ask you for your advice. I must admit that I continue to struggle with that one. My step-daughters have taught me more about being a great horseman than they will ever know.

The Death of a Dream

I never officially graduated the Horse Science program. I find it ironic that I am sitting here writing a book when I am one Composition credit shy of an Associate's degree. However, I did not feel as though having that piece of paper to hang on my wall was going to make or break my career as a colt starter. In 1997, I made the decision to quit school and hang my shingle out as a local horse trainer.

I had a friend who owned a boarding facility. We worked out a business deal. I could use his facility to grow my business. He collected the money for board on my client's horses and I charged a separate fee for training. I tried for five years to create a successful business as a colt starter. During that time, I had the privilege of starting about ten colts a year. Most of these horses were pretty straight forward and easy to get under saddle. However, there were a handful I really wasn't prepared for and my time with them increased my fears that began with the little mustang in college. Two more trips to the emergency room caused me to realize that my dream had turned into my nightmare. I started to dread going to the barn every day. I would make excuses and soon started asking the barn owner for his his help with my training horses. He would eventually take over the training business and I decided that I would get a "real" job and only keep my personal horses for recreation. My dream died.

It was extremely painful, and I recall feeling a sense of surrender to a life that was not going to be filled with passion, but with a daily drudgery of doing whatever it takes to pay the bills. A piece of my heart shriveled. I would go through several jobs trying to find one that didn't make me miserable. I worked as a fork lift operator in a factory for around 18 months. I delivered the mail and even worked as a school bus driver. Each day at any one of these jobs was torture. I knew that I had so much more to offer the world than just an eight-hour shift. I wanted to make a difference and feel as though I had something unique and special to bring to the table. All I needed to do those jobs was to be able to fog a mirror. I refer to those as the dark years. I believe that you can only fully appreciate the light when you have experienced some of the dark. I am very motivated to never go back to just doing what it takes to pay the bills. Because of the pain and discontent I felt during those years, I am committed to filling each day with my passion. I work each day to be great at what I do so that I can live a life of fulfillment and joy, and not just getting by.

My Prince Charming: Rocky

One of the first gifts given to me by my husband was a horse. We had been dating for about a year and I was about to "graduate" from college. I did not have a horse of my own and I was desperate for one. Shane agreed to help me. I was looking for a two year old that hadn't been started under saddle yet. I was about to become a professional colt starter and I felt as though I needed to start one of my own so that I could use that horse as advertisement for my business. I wanted something athletic and dramatic looking. I searched for several weeks before I found just what I was looking for.

He was a two-year-old leopard Appaloosa. I fell in love with him the moment we met. The day I met Rocky, he was in a pasture with two other young horses. When I went to meet him, the woman who sold him to me gave a whistle and all three horses came galloping to the gate. The other two horses were fairly plain and did nothing dramatic on their way to see us, but Rocky was proud and majestic. He raced to us with his head high and tail in the air. As he reached us, he pranced, snorted, and showed off. My heart raced and I knew instantly that I had found the partner I was looking for. He would become my prince charming.

Rocky was boarded at the same facility where I had tried to grow a horse training business. The day I moved him to our friends' barn was the day he earned the name Rocky. We turned him out in a paddock by himself so that he could get used to his environment before introducing him to any of the other horses. He immediately began striking and squealing at one of the more dominant horses across a gate. The barn owner and I began were concerned that one or both of the horses would end up with a leg tangled in the gate and in a terrible wreck. We decided to open the gate and just let them sort out their dominance issues. That was when the two really started to have it out. They were fighting just like the wild mustang stallions I had seen on National Geographic videos. They reared up at each other and knelt down to bite at each other's knees. Both looking for the other to yield and therefor claim the role of herd leader. I was terrified that Rocky was going to get hurt. The other gelding was a great deal bigger and was already the herd leader. Rocky didn't back down. All we could do was stand back and let them sort things out. By the time they finished, they were great friends and mutually grooming each other. The older gelding won that battle, but Rocky had earned the right to be in his herd.

Getting Rocky under saddle using the methods explained by Parelli Natural Horsemanship went pretty smoothly. We bonded very quickly and I spent every spare moment with him. I rode him successfully for over a year until the day fate would change everything forever. I had arrived at the barn in the early afternoon just as I had done hundreds of times before. The barn owner's wife is my good friend and I intended to visit with her before I played with Rocky. As I got out of the car, I looked for him. He was standing near the fence and nickered to me. Nothing looked out of place so I called out to say hello and told him I would be out to play with him soon. I went inside and visited with my friend for around thirty minutes. When I went back outside Rocky had not moved. I remember thinking that was unusual.

I went to him with the intention of bringing him in and getting him ready for a ride. But, as I got close I saw one of the most horrific sights I had ever seen in my life. The fence that Rocky was behind was something that is called high tensile wire. It is a steel wire pulled very tight. Rocky's hind leg was woven between the many strands of wire and his flesh was hanging from the bone. I could literally see the large bone in his lower leg and the groves that the wire had put in it. Rocky must have lied down near the fence and got his leg through. Then, he probably got up and felt panicked by being trapped in the fence. Horses are naturally claustrophobic because their natural defense is flight. He pulled hard enough to break the 6 inch wooden corner post that was about thirty yards away from where he was. He was standing calmly now and looking to me for assistance. I had a moment where I wanted to panic and loose my mind, but I gathered my thoughts and raced to the house for help. The barn owner got the horse trailer ready for the trip the horse hospital while my friend and I cut Rocky out of the fence with wire cutters.

He loaded onto the small trailer like a champion and we raced to the hospital. The prognosis was pretty grim. The wire had completely severed the tendon that Rocky used to move his hoof as well as punctured a joint sack in a major joint. What all of that meant was that Rocky was not likely to ever be 100% sound again. I was devastated. My whole life revolved around this horse. The next decision I had to make was did I want to spend the thousands of dollars and months that it would take to heal his wounds with no guarantee that he would ever get back to a quality of life that was humane? Or did I want to end his suffering? It was an impossible choice, but I could not bear the thought of not at least giving him a chance to try and heal. So, I made a commitment to him. I would keep trying as long as he kept trying.

Rocky spent six more weeks in the hospital on IV antibiotics and complete stall rest. I visited him every day. After that, he would come home, but have to remain on complete stall rest for another six months. We needed him to move as little as possible. I had to change his bandages every day during that time. Horses are designed by nature to move up to ten miles a day. Most horses forced to do that much stall rest would develop a type of mental illness that horse trainers call vices. Horses will do things like weave back and forth the way an orphan baby does when he doesn't get held enough. They will paw at the walls or become agitated. Rocky never did any of that. He was patient and calm, always. He would often lie down in his stall to rest. I would go and lie with him and just cry over the lost potential. I felt such guilt for not protecting him and keeping him safe. My heart was broken.

It would take eighteen months before Rocky would be well enough to be ridden again. He actually got to a spot where I thought he was going to be okay. I was riding him again and learning a great deal from him. Then, about two and a half years after his accident, he started to show signs of lameness in the opposite hind leg. The vet diagnosed him with degenerative arthritis and informed me that he was never going to be 100% or even 80% again. I still feel sad when I think of how great we could have been together. My relationship with this horse was easy and natural. We truly enjoyed each other's company and he will forever hold a special place in my heart. He is now helping a friend of mine with her riding confidence. He is now her prince charming. Everything happens for a reason. If Rocky had never gotten hurt, I would have never met my next great teacher.

My Savior: Maxi

It took several weeks, but I came to accept Rocky was not going to be the partner I needed for my business. I love him unconditionally and was devoted to him no matter what. But, I began to look for a new horse that would be athletic enough to help me achieve my goals. Shane and I had our own place and we were boarding a few horses for friends. One of those friends had just purchased a black and white paint yearling. He was gorgeous, playful, outgoing, and he was going to be HUGE! I fell in love with him instantly. I was disappointed to find out that his human was not interested in selling him to me, so I called her horse's breeder to inquire about the next year's foal crop.

I told the breeder of my attraction to the young gelding and asked her if she had bred that gelding's mother back to the same stallion. She informed me that she had and so I placed an order. I told her that I wanted a filly (a female) and that she must be black and white. I wanted her to have a similar personality to her brother. And lastly she needed to have enough white to qualify for regular paint horse papers. If you don't have enough white, the horse gets registered as a solid paint. Solid paint papers generally means that the horse is less valuable. But I didn't want her to have so much white it would be overpowering.

The following spring, the breeder called me to inform me that my horse had been born the night before. I immediately rushed to the farm to meet her. She was everything that I had asked for and more. She and her mother were in a foaling stall. Maxi was just twelve hours old. I anxiously peaked my head over the half wall inside the dilapidated barn to see her and fell in love instantly. She marched boldly over to me as if to say, "Who are you, and what do you want?"

I knew from that moment that she was meant to be with me and that we would do great things together. I made arrangements to buy her that day. She had to stay with her mom for the first 5 months of her life, but she has been my girl from the moment we met. I would visit her at the breeding farm several times a week. And was over the moon the day I finally got to bring her home. She instantly made herself at home with my herd and she has been with me ever since.

CHAPTER 4

Making a Change

A Lesson With Linda

AFTER LOSING MY confidence for colt starting, I tried several different ways to support my horsey habit with "real" jobs. I worked in a factory for 18 months. I delivered the mail, and even drove a school bus. I was miserable in all of these jobs and longed to do something more meaningful with my life. I am an intense individual and I feel things to the extreme. As an extrovert, I have a tendency to infect my environment with whatever I am feeling. So, life in my home was pretty unhappy during much of those years and it took a toll on my marriage and family. I was searching for something. My husband and I often refer to this time as the dark years. I found what I was looking for in 2004.

I was studying the Parelli program with my own horses at home. I had become a member of their Savvy Club. With my membership came access to an opportunity to apply to get to do a lesson with Linda Parelli (one of the company's directors) at a seminar they were hosting near my home in Council Bluffs, IA. Maxi and I were chosen and got to spend 2 hours with Linda in front of a crowd of about 2,000 people. I was having trouble keeping Maxi motivated and responsive and was excited for the help. Linda was very gracious and I will never be able to thank her enough for the spark she ignited that day.

I learned more about myself, my horsemanship, and what was possible in those two hours than I had in the previous ten years. Linda is an amazing teacher with just the right balance of push for progress and positive reinforcement to build confidence. My dream of becoming a horse professional was reborn. I could see that with Parelli Natural Horsemanship, I could stay safe, have fun, and stick to my principles as well as create a financially rewarding business.

At this seminar, I spoke with the director of the Parelli professionals program, Neil. He explained to me the steps to becoming a Parelli professional. What really stands out about my conversation with Neil was that he said that in order for me to make it in this industry I was going to have to want it more than I wanted air. I remember at the time thinking that was strange thing to say. How can you want something more than air? I would later find out. With the support of my husband and family, I jumped in the deep end head first.

Running Off To Join The Circus

Level three in the Parelli home study program was the first milestone that I needed to achieve in order to fulfill my dream of becoming an instructor. Level three in horsemanship terms was a little like becoming a high school graduate. I wanted to get there as quickly as possible, so I signed up for an intensive ten-week course at the Florida center in 2005. This course was called "The School" and was promoted as a course that could help you accelerate your results. That was *exactly* what I was looking for! At the time I thought ten whole weeks of horsemanship immersion should be long enough to get to level three. I had only just achieved level one in the program and my horse was only four years old at the time. A lot of folks within the Parelli program had advised me that level three in ten weeks might be an unrealistic goal (a bit like trying to skip from seventh grade to graduation in one year). But, of course, that only made me more determined. The best way to get me to do something is for someone to tell me that they don't think that I can.

Level three was one hurdle, but financing my education was another. The course cost $1,000 per week, not to mention the travel and lodging costs. I was not in a financial position to be able to just write a check. I did, however, have two other assets that would help me. One was a husband who has been financially responsible his whole life and therefor has great credit. The other was enough heart and desire to keep searching for a way to make this dream come true. I believe if you want something badly enough you will find a way, otherwise you will just find excuses. My passion and commitment to my desired outcome helped me to convince my husband that it was worth risking our assets to borrow the money. I am so thankful that he has always believed in me and has been willing to take risks for my benefit. Borrowing the money to finance my education would eventually prove to be another challenge. We had enough equity in our home to be eligible for the money. Convincing our bank to lend us the money was surprisingly easy. Although, the pressure of that looming debt would later prove to be a significant trial in my journey. By November of 2004 I had the money and had been accepted into "The School". Arrangements were made and I was on my way.

Shane and I arrived at the Parelli campus in Reddick, Florida in January of 2005. I was so anxious to get started that I was the first student to arrive. The Florida campus is magical. There are huge live oak trees dripping with Spanish moss. If you arrive early in the morning a haze from the dew lingers over everything. I had never seen anything like it. The big beautiful green trees and the bluish moss gave the campus an enchanted feel. I knew as we pulled in on the first day that this was going to be one of the most important things I would do with my life. Just being there on campus felt magical. I did not know what I would learn would be way more than horsemanship.

I had a lot riding on being successful in this course and I was determined to get my money's worth. I am an intense student. I made a promise to my husband that our investment would be worth the risk. Every day I would arrive early enough to feed my horse before breakfast and be the last one to leave at the end of the day. I *needed* to achieve level three during this course. So, I did not waste a single minute. We were in class all day and I spent all of my spare time before and after class as well as during breaks studying the theory. It was during one of those study sessions that my first life lesson through horsemanship began to brew.

We were supposed to take the weekends to rest and soak on what we learned during the week. I had people counting on me to succeed and I was not going to waste a single minute on relaxing. One Saturday morning I was studying the level three theory guide as I was having breakfast in the lodge. I came to a section in this booklet in which Pat Parelli tells us to watch our thoughts, for they become our words. "Choose your words carefully, for they become actions. Understand your actions, for they become habits. Study your habits, for they will become your character. Develop your character, for it becomes your destiny." A horseman's thoughts are positive, progressive and natural. For some reason on that day, that information had a profound impact. The, "Be careful of your thoughts" began to swirl around in my head and torment me.

After breakfast, I went out to get some tasks checked off of my level three list. I was going to work on the FreeStyle riding patterns that were required for passing level 3. Our instructor had informed the class earlier that week that Pat Parelli's standard for these patterns was to have your horse so responsive that you could fold your arms, guiding your horse with your body language. So, of course, I intended to do the most complicated pattern called a Clover Leaf. I also intended to do it at the canter with my arms folded. This would be a bit like asking a second grader who had just learned basic addition and subtraction to understand and calculate trigonometry. It should have occurred to me to allow myself and my horse Maxi to learn this pattern with her walking, using my reins for clarification. At the walk we both would have had the time and space to see that there was a pattern occurring. However, I wanted quick results and I was going to make this pattern happen at the canter today!

Maxi is very confident in herself and not very motivated to move her feet. In the Parelli program we would describe her as a left brain introvert. This means that she is a low energy horse who doesn't like to be told what to do. Asking her to canter the Cloverleaf pattern at this point in our education was a bit like asking a tortoise to run a four minute mile. Being forceful and too direct is the worst strategy to have with this kind of horse. It is my belief that the world would be a better place if all of our leaders were required to achieve level four in the Parelli Natural Horsemanship program with a left brain introverted horse before they could run for office. The role of leader is diligently earned with these horses moment by moment and is never handed over undeserved. You have to learn to see things from this horse's point of view and get them in the mood to do what you are asking for before they are going to be willing to do it. If you are in the mindset of just making a left brain horse do what you want, you will get some negative feedback (like bucking) and are not likely to achieve your desired outcomes. I did not yet understand that about my horse. All I was focused on was getting to level three. I wasn't really thinking about my horse's needs.

It wasn't long before we were both sweaty and breathing hard. It was a pretty ugly scene. The entire time I was torturing my horse with the clover leaf pattern, I was hearing in my head, "be careful of your thoughts" over and over again. Finally, I reached a breaking point. I was frustrated and so was my horse. This was not the way it was supposed to go. What I was doing to my horse was not the dream I had in my heart. I stopped my horse and shouted out loud, "Okay, what are my thoughts?!?!". Luckily, it was just me and Maxi and there was no one else around to see my moment of madness.

Because of my childhood, I was carrying around a huge chip on my shoulder. I was holding a grudge towards my parents and had been for nearly fifteen years. I got a raw deal as a kid and the only way I thought I could forgive them was if they begged me for forgiveness. I knew that those thoughts weren't healthy and that they were hurting me. I just didn't know how to let go of them. I had become so angry and hard for so long that it had just become who I was at the time. In that moment with my horse, I realized that those thoughts were keeping me from achieving my dreams with horses. A horseman is positive, progressive and natural, not bitter and self-absorbed. If I didn't let go of my anger and resentment, I was never going to be the human that my horse was dreaming of. *She* needed me to let go of those thoughts. I wanted to be extraordinary with horses and achieve things that were above and beyond average horsemanship skills. On that hill that day, my horse taught me how to forgive my parents. It was through my extreme desire to achieve outstanding results with my horse that I could change my thoughts. Maxi gave me the ability to forgive. It was an amazing gift that I will never be able to thank her enough for. I felt as though the weight of the world had been lifted from my shoulders. It was so remarkable that I proceeded to tell my story to everyone who would sit still long enough.

I have since come to understand that there was nothing to forgive my parents for. They, as all parents, were only doing the best that they could with the tools they had available to them at the time. I love my mother and father deeply. I continue to focus on the gifts that they have given me and only allow my brain to focus on our happy times together. That lesson has served me in all of my relationships, including the relationship I have with myself. I will be eternally grateful to my horse for that lesson. She is an incredible teacher and I look forward to all that she has to teach me about becoming the best me that I can be.

Walking Your Talk

Maxi and I had a nickname during our first course at the Florida Parelli center. It was "Bucky". If you ever needed to find her and me, all you needed to do was look for the cloud of dust and listen for the sound of my voice cursing her. This is why I am glad that my first horse to level four was a left brain introvert (LBI). She was not going to tolerate bossiness, inconsiderate treatment or direct line thinking. I would tell her to do something and she would say with her body language, "what if I don't?". And my general response would be, "If you don't, I will whack you." She, of course, is way better than me at the whacking game. She would rear, buck, star jump, strike, anything she could think of to try and help me understand that I was on the wrong track. I did not understand at the time that I was causing that behavior. I wanted to blame her and would most often get into huge arguments with her, hence, the nickname. It wasn't until several years later that I came to appreciate that folks were not just calling my horse Bucky. That was my nickname as well. Hmmm, how interesting.

The first time I started to realize how one-sided our conversations were was the day that we learned about thresholds (the limit of what my horse is capable of handling with confidence) and how to discover them. It was the day that I learned how to play a game called "me and my shadow" that I realized that I had never asked Maxi what her opinion was. On this day, we were asked to just suggest that our horses go somewhere and then we were meant to follow them. This is an exercise that is meant to help you to walk a mile in your horse's horseshoes. Maxi headed down a route that we had taken every day for the last four or five weeks. We traveled about 400 yards. In that space, she had thirty-seven thresholds. I had never noticed or acknowledged a single one prior to that day. I had no idea what she was going through. My confidence and ambition were hiding the fact that she was unconfident. She could go if I was micromanaging her. But, I had never instilled any self confidence in her. I couldn't believe it. I was devastated and so ashamed of my lack of awareness.

During the following days we learned another game that exposed the poor quality of communication between me and Maxi. We learned how to take a passenger lesson, which is just like me and my shadow, except we were riding our horses now. I had never allowed my horse to tell me her opinion before, let alone encouraged her to. When I asked her what she wanted to do, she didn't know. She would just turn and look at me as if to say, "What do you want me to do?". We would spend entire afternoons just spinning in circles. She didn't know how to have an opinion or express her desires to me because I had never created a space that was safe for her to do that.

That lesson needed to soak for several weeks. It wasn't until I was in my second ten-week course that I really made a change. I had an instructor ask me if I thought I was walking my talk. I didn't really know what she meant at first. She followed up with, are you doing everything with savvy? Savvy is a word that Pat Parelli uses to describe the skills and habits required by both horse and human to have a good relationship. When she asked if I was doing everything with savvy she was asking if I was using the relationship skills that I was learning for horses with everyone in my life. You see horses are excellent at seeing when someone is using a technique, but hasn't made a change in their heart. The only way for those skills to become habit would be for me to use them all of the time.

Then, it hit me like a ton of bricks. Maxi was not the only individual in my life that I was talking over. My upbringing and my natural personality had me believing that the only individual I can truly count on was me. That belief combined with my intense desire to succeed in the Parelli program was causing me to be chauvinistic, not just with my horse, but with my fellow students, family, and friends. I finally came to realize that more times than not, Maxi had really great ideas. But I was missing them because I never gave her an opportunity to share them with me. I was tripping over dollars to pick up pennies.

It wasn't until I started practicing what I learned from that lesson with all of the people in my life that I really came to understand how much I was missing out on. I am married to the greatest man on the planet. He has supported me through forty weeks of courses at the Parelli campuses in both Florida and Colorado as a student; six months touring all over the country with Pat and Linda as a member of the behind-the-scenes crew; and nearly three years as a member of the faculty teaching full-time at the Parelli Centers all over the world. I have gotten to go to the UK, Dubai, Sweden, and Australia and all over this great country of ours. All while he stayed at home to hold down the fort. I would not have been capable of sticking with it without his love, support, and belief in me. I believe that Maxi is the reason that I am still married to this incredible man. If she hadn't taught me the strength that comes from being vulnerable and appreciating the synergy that happens when you allow your communication to be two or more individuals sharing and understanding an idea, I might not still have the privilege of being able to call myself Mrs. Shane Smith. I needed to become a better listener and it took Maxi being so persistent with me to learn that. She is truly a gift. If she had been a more fearful horse, I would have been able to get a lot done by just being bossy. Thank goodness that she is so opinionated!

Pat tells us that your horse is your mirror; he means that your horse is reflecting to you the quality of your communication and ability to be in a true partnership with mutual responsibilities. We often can't rely on other humans for that kind of feedback because humans have a tendency to include their own agenda and ego in their responses. However, the horse cannot help but be in the moment and give honest feedback. Maxi inspires me to seek out the best me that I can be. She has very high standards and continues to help me learn about myself and to grow as a human being. I have to admit that I still have days where I slip into old habits. But Maxi continues to increase my awareness and helps me get back on track.

At What Cost

The greatest resources available to people studying the Parelli program are the people and staff who have dedicated their lives to studying and sharing the program as a profession. Parelli Natural

Horsemanship has some truly amazing people within the organization who are compassionate, caring, knowledgeable, and dedicated to serving our mission. Our mission is to make the world a better place for horses and the humans who love them. My instructors for my first course are without a doubt two of the best that Parelli has to offer. One of the most important bits of wisdom they had to share was for us to keep everything in perspective and balanced with the rest of our lives.

I had peers that had gone to great extremes to get themselves into this course. I myself had borrowed money against my home. I had friends who had sold their homes and maxed out their credit cards to finance their education. I had friends who had dissolved their marriages in order to get their education. I have even heard it said that more people have gotten divorced in the pursuit of becoming a Parelli professional than people in the military. I think that once you start experiencing the emotions that come from feeling successful with your horse it becomes addictive and it is easy to slip into obsession. Our horses start to meet our basic human needs for consistency, variety, significance, connection, growth, and contribution. When you allow a horse and the Parelli program to meet those needs on a greater level than your two-legged loved ones, then it only makes sense that one would start to distance themselves from those who are not meeting those needs. I made a decision at the beginning of this crazy journey that there was one price I was not willing to pay for my career—my marriage. There have been times when it seemed as though my husband and I were on separate paths and that this journey was going to cost me my relationship with him. But luckily, the relationship skills we are learning for our horses also apply to our human relationships. I have had dozens of outstanding mentors in this area along the way. And my husband and I continue to stay committed to each other.

I completed that ten week course as a level two graduate which is kind of like graduating middle school. Unfortunately, I had only passed about one-third of level three. I had convinced Shane that I would come home from this course with my level three in hand. So not achieving that did make me feel like a failure. I was not ready to give up and I immediately signed up for the next ten week school happening on the Parelli campus in Pagosa Springs, Colorado.

My Thoughts Create My World

My husband delivered me to the Parelli campus in Pagosa Springs in April of 2005 with renewed hope and enthusiasm for my goals, but also a fear that my classmates would treat me differently because I had a relationship with our instructor. She had been my instructor in my previous course and had always believed in me and had been very encouraging. I was worried that our having a prior relationship would cause the other students to feel resentful and subconsciously I made sure that they did. Our first day of class began with introductions and an outline of the course. It was a beautiful sunny morning and so we sat in a circle outside around the fire pit and introduced ourselves and told a little story about why we were there. When it came to be my turn, our instructor introduced me as a future Parelli professional and was very complimentary. Those words did not go unnoticed by the rest of the group. And I proceeded to make things worse. Our instructor needed to retrieve something from her office. After she left, one of the other students called me a teacher's pet. He was joking, but I took it personally and verbally lashed out. I announced to the whole group, "I am here to achieve my horsemanship goals and I care a great deal more what she (our instructor) thinks of me than what any of you think of me." This single proclamation would set the tone for me for the following ten weeks and would later become a great lesson in choosing my words more wisely. What most of my peers heard me say was, "I don't care what you think of me. I only care what she thinks." That one moment of my brain to mouth filter malfunctioning would prevent me from making some friends and would inspire a few folks in the course to treat me unkindly. I would over the course of ten weeks, have many private cry sessions over it.

My biggest highlight from this course would be the day that Pat Parelli (my hero and mentor) told me he liked my horse. It was on a Saturday morning. I was, of course, at the center trying to develop the skills that I still needed for passing my level 3. I was in an area called the playground riding my horse, Maxi. This area is full of obstacles and challenges that we use to develop our communication with our horses. I had paused for a moment and was thinking about what I should do next when Pat's son Caton came whizzing by in a golf cart. He did not stop and continued on in the direction of a pasture where several of Pat's horses lived. I remember thinking that Pat had probably asked him to retrieve one or more of those horses. As soon as Caton was out of sight, he was out of mind. Several minutes later, I sighted another golf cart. Only, this one solicited a very different emotion, panic. It was Mr. Pat Parelli himself. Even though I had been studying his program for years, and had been a student at his centers for many weeks, I had never had any one-on-one interaction with him. I was terrified! I would imagine it would be a pretty similar experience as one of Oprah's staff members who don't have daily interaction with her encountering her in the cafeteria or bathroom. I was the only person in the playground and I was praying that he was too busy to stop and talk. But he immediately zeroed in on me and headed straight for me and Maxi. I froze. I figured that if I was just sitting on my horse, petting her, I couldn't possibly be doing anything stupid or wrong.

When Pat reached us he asked me if I had seen his son. I replied, "Yes, about five minutes ago he headed towards the pasture with your horses in it." He thanked me and then asked, "Is that your horse?". I replied, "Yes, sir." He then said, "I can evaluate a horse's quality in just a few seconds and I like your horse." My mind began to whirl! Pat Parelli just said that he likes my horse!!! I squeaked out a thank you and he drove away. It was one of the greatest moments of my life! My mentor and hero had just complimented my horse! I spent the next several days recanting that story to anyone who would hold still long enough to hear it. I called my mother, husband, and friends excitedly recalling the day that Pat Parelli said that he liked my horse.

Several days later one of Pat's most respected and experienced instructors, David arrived at the center. I was eager to meet him and one of my fellow students and friend had a personal relationship with this instructor. I asked him to introduce us. As we chatted casually, my friend suggested that I tell David what Pat had said about my horse. I told him the story and his response was, "Oh ya, we tell students that we like their horses all of the time." I was crushed! He was insinuating that Pat's compliment had been insincere.

Later that day I was in the lodge, where students and staff have their meals, telling the story of how the David had taken the wind out of my sails to one of my friends. As I finished the story and turned to walk away, I was facing him. I could see that he felt bad and he apologized profusely. I light-heartedly teased him about the mean spiritedness of his words. "Couldn't you just allow me to believe that Pat truly likes my horse?" He apologized again and our playful, but mildly awkward conversation ended.

Later that day, I was playing with my horse in the playground when David approached me and Maxi. He asked if she was the horse Pat had complimented. I informed him that she was. He proceeded to compliment her, repeatedly proclaiming how wonderful she was. I pretended to not accept his compliments and this interaction would become the source of a private joke between me and him for the remainder of his stay. Even now when I see him, if I am with Maxi he will say, "HEY! Nice horse!"

This ten-week course would prove to be even more difficult than my first ten-week School. Aside from the discomfort of having created a hostile relationship with several of my classmates and an intensified feeling of homesickness, I still did not pass my level three. There were just a few tasks that I was missing by the end of the course, and I was extremely frustrated and disappointed. I applied to attend the following professionals' course anyway. And, because I had spent so much time at the centers already, I was allowed to attend that course even though I had not passed my level three. The invitation to the course titled "The University" was bittersweet. I was excited to go, but felt as though I had cheated. To me, the rules were clear and I did not meet the criteria. But I applied my signature determination to finishing my level three during that course and catching up with the rest of the class as soon as possible.

"The University": Not Everyone is a Fan

The next ten weeks became a time for me to truly understand what I am made of. I had great tests of fortitude through horsemanship, but the greater challenge would come with professional evaluations and life. Pat Parelli has ten criteria that he evaluates future Parelli professionals by so that each student knows where their strengths and weaknesses are. I had been evaluated by these criteria during my 10-week schools and had always done well. The instructors in the course give each student a score of one to ten on each criterion every three or four weeks. You must achieve at least a seven to be considered "passing". My feedback in the school had been, "You are exactly what this program is looking for. Just keep doing what you are doing." I was given eights and nines on all criteria at every evaluation. Tens are very rarely given as that would mean that you have no room for improvement.

All that praise came to an abrupt halt in my first evaluation in the university. After about three weeks, we had our first set of interviews. We would each be marched into the office to hear the thoughts and feedback of both our instructor as well as the dean of the schools. It was a pretty intense environment and I was on the verge of tears before we even started. I didn't really know why. It was just that I had so much riding on this and I really wanted to do well. I remember that the room we were in seemed to shrink the moment I sat down. Everything just seemed too close. I felt my throat start to close and I was breathing as deeply as I could so that I wouldn't start crying before we even started. It didn't take long before there would be no holding back the tears. I was given mostly threes and fours and was told, "You are a round peg trying to shove yourself in a square hole." Whoa! That stung! They also told me that they could read my body language and be able to tell if I was having a good day or a bad day from a mile away, which was not necessarily a bad thing, but that maybe I should do something that would allow me to have a few more good days and a few less bad days. I was completely caught off guard and totally devastated. I had no idea that I was so far off track. They even went so far as to say that maybe I should consider that I was in the wrong place. I knew that being evaluated in the university would be on a much tougher scale than in the school. But, that meeting really knocked the wind out of me. I was flooded with so many emotions that all I could do was stare at my evaluators and try not to have a complete mental episode. "This cannot be happening," I thought to myself. "How could I be so far off track?"

I left that meeting completely overwhelmed. What was I going to do now? I had convinced my husband that I could do this and that it was worth risking our future to get me here. I felt as though my whole world was crashing down around me. Everything that I had dreamed for myself and my future was falling apart. I had already spent over twenty weeks and tens of thousands of dollars. Luckily, I was supremely privileged to have a friend in that course that would help me to take that feedback and be better for it. Today, I am thankful for that review. Those words would become an intense motivator for me. Those people in that room did not know me well enough to make those kinds of assessments. I hadn't shown them the best of me yet and I made it my mission to prove them wrong. I could either feel sorry for myself or I could make an epic come back. Don't get me wrong, I spent a good twenty-four hours feeling sorry for myself. And that evening I drank copious amounts of tequila. But there was more on the line here, than my ego. My family was counting on me, and I was not about to let them down. Pat has high standards for his professionals. That is why I wanted to be one. If it were easy, then it wouldn't be so coveted. I just needed to adjust my course. Evaluation meetings still get me emotional. It has been years since I had one that was so awful, but somehow, I still go in fighting back tears. Linda Parelli has told me that it is just my passion leaking out. I try to hang on to those words so that I do not feel embarrassed or ashamed for getting so emotional.

Conquering My Fears

During my ten weeks in the university I also had multiple opportunities to face some old fears. My college and colt starting experiences had not only dinged my confidence as a rider, but also my confidence in instructors. Trust is very difficult for me, and when it comes to horsemanship it is essential that a person have faith and trust in the people and horses that are directing your journey.

During my first week in the Uni I got assigned to the team that brought the horses in from the 200 acre pasture every morning to be fed and prepared for their training sessions that day. We called it jingling. That may sound like a simple enough task. However, this particular chore was done horseback at sunrise. And the 200 acre pasture was more like a 200 acre mountain. Every morning when I would step up onto Maxi just as the sun was coming over the horizon I felt like a real horseman. I was in the San Juan Mountains, using my horse to do a real job. It was incredible. But, the second we would start to head out, I would find myself really doubting myself and my horse. That would cause me to start micromanaging her and she would, indeed, get nervous. The worst part would was that I knew that I was causing my own troubles. I just needed to have a little more faith in her. But somehow I just couldn't manage it. I did have a few incidents that increased my fears.

The very first day we went out to do this would be my first opportunity to lose confidence. As we were riding out we were given some information on herding horses. The first thing we were told was what position we would have. The lead rider was meant to set the pace. Then a couple of riders would ride in the middle to keep the herd from bottle necking anywhere. And finally, there would be several riders bringing up the rear of the herd. I was to ride in the rear position on my first day. Initially, it seemed as though that would be the easiest position to be in. However, the rear riders are meant to match the pace of the herd, no matter what. That was easy enough until we got to what was known as the jingle hill.

The jingle hill makes me think of *The Man From Snowy* River scene where the rider goes galloping over an impossible-to-ride precipice. It was very narrow and steep. After the herd reached the top of the hill they could see the pens and their awaiting breakfast down below. Their enthusiasm could not be contained and despite the heroic efforts of the lead rider, the herd began to gallop down the jingle hill! I was terrified. Maxi began to prance and dance with the excitement that the herd was generating. The rider behind me tried to get me to just allow her to run with the herd. "Are you crazy? I can't!", I responded. It was one of the most terrifying experiences in my life. Over the course of the next ten weeks, I would learn to be able to deal with the jingle hill, but I cannot say that I ever gained confidence. I do believe that experience set me on a path that would lead to the feedback I received in my evaluations. You see, I am the type of person that when I am afraid, it often looks as though I am angry. I spent a great deal of those ten weeks very afraid and so looking very angry. I still had so much work to do on myself. I did not gain faith and trust in that course. But, I did gain awareness.

Horsey Healing

I paid a great price for my education. I spent a great deal of money as well as time away from home and family. The biggest price I paid was that of lost moments. While I was in the University, my grandmother passed away suddenly. She hadn't been sick. I had no warning that she was close to passing. I was at the center in Pagosa

Springs, CO when someone from the Parelli office tracked me down. They informed me that my mother had been trying to reach me and that it was urgent that I call her immediately. I knew something bad had happened. My mom doesn't call me very often, and she had never before insisted that I call her right away. I went to the barn and called her, bracing myself for bad news. It was a short phone call. She informed me that my grandmother had passed and that I had two days to get home for the funeral.

I was in shock. I was again feeling confused and unsure of what to feel. My grandmother was a very kind and loving woman. But, I had not spent much time with her in my life. I did not know her well. But, the little time I did get with her was quality time. My mom, my grandma, and I would sit down over a cup of hot chocolate and talk about all kinds of things. I loved those talks and soon began to realize how much I was going to miss them.

I walked out of the barn with a heavy heart and tears in my eyes. I needed a hug. My friend was playing with her horse not far from the barn. I walked to her to tell her what had just happened and to seek some comfort. We stood close and she pulled me in to hug me and give me a shoulder to cry on. As we stood there in each other's arms grieving the loss of my grandmother, my friend's horse came over and wrapped her head and neck around us. It was an extremely spiritual and healing moment in my life. Something magical happened that afternoon. I believe that my grandma had something to do with it.

Tail Between My Legs

By the end of the summer of 2005, I had spent thirty weeks at the Parelli Centers as a student trying to achieve level three horsemanship. I had experienced a great deal and learned more than I had bargained for. I had gone to the heights of praise and success, but also the lows of evaluation and perceived failures. It had been a roller coaster ride and that emotional whirlwind lasted through the very last day. On the last day of class, I still clung to the hope that I would be awarded my level three and therefor join the ranks of Parelli professionals.

That morning our instructor took the entire class on a trail ride that went to a place called "Paradise Meadows." This trail ride was not just a leisurely stroll through the woods. This was a mountain ride with switchbacks and steep narrow trails. It was beautiful, but not laid-back. About half way to the top, a mountain thunderstorm rolled in. The skies darkened in a matter of minutes and the temperature dropped at least 10 degrees almost instantly. It came quick and with a great deal of force. This storm brought with it pounding and drenching rain as well as a forceful wind. We found a place along the trail to hunker down and wait it out. People were complaining, panicking, and a few even took it upon themselves to head back down the trail to make their way back to the ranch. I watched how our instructor handle the situation and did my best to handle myself in the same manner that she did. She just pulled her hat down low and her collar up high and began to wait the storm out. Lucky for us those types of storms generally blow out as quickly as they blew in. It only lasted about fifteen minutes. We were drenched, but unharmed and continued up the trail. Man was it worth it. The view took my breath away. You could see for miles down into this lush green valley. The sun was shining and the sky was the most incredible shade of bright blue. It would be one of the greatest moments of the summer for me.

On our way back, I was still holding tight to the idea that I might be awarded my level three at the graduation ceremony later that evening. I wasn't going to accept defeat until I was driving back home over Wolf Creek Pass. My husband had come to help drive me home and

I was glad to have him there for such a special and important day in my life. That evening we walked to the lodge hand-in-hand, hopeful and excited about our future. During the ceremony our instructor would recall highlights from the previous ten weeks and the things that she had learned. Several of the other students would stand up and do the same. Certificates of completion were handed out and that was the end of it. No level three for me and of course no instructor certification. I was embarrassed because I had convinced my husband and myself that I was going to get my level three that night. I was discouraged because I had given everything I had to give at the time and it didn't seem to be enough. And, I was angry. I wanted it so badly and I had worked so hard. I had spent thousands of dollars and sacrificed thirty weeks of my life to be there to achieve my dream of becoming a Parelli professional. And that evening I felt as though it had all been for nothing. As my husband and I drove away the next day with Maxi in tow, I was not sure that I would be back. My spirit was damaged and my confidence was low.

CHAPTER 5

Not Ready to Give Up

I LEFT THE Parelli Center that summer with my tail tucked between my legs for sure. Before I took my first course, I thought for sure that I would just sail through the whole process. I had been riding horses my whole life. My mom likes to say that I have been riding since before I was born because she was riding when she was pregnant with me. I came from two horse families. I spent two years studying the business of horses in college. I had a great horse and was full of confidence. But everything happens for a reason and after several weeks of feeling sorry for myself, I recommitted to my dream.

At that time, Linda Parelli was developing a new strategy for how to teach the Parelli Program. And with Pat's guidance and the guidance of a woman who specializes in adult learning, Linda developed a new course that would be offered on the Parelli Campuses. Due to the drastic changes in teaching philosophy, this new course became mandatory for all current and future Parelli Professionals. Without my level 3 I could not attend another University course, but I was eligible for this course and signed up for it as soon as I could. The debt I was incurring was becoming significant. But, all along I had people telling me that my earning potential as a Parelli professional was in the six figure range. If I couldn't earn that within the first couple of years, then I wasn't trying very hard. So, I tried not to think about the debt and continued to work on my horsemanship. After all, Pat had told us, if you take care of your horsemanship, your horsemanship will take care of you. So, I returned to the Florida Parelli campus in January of 2006 ready to learn more and focused on achieving level three. Little did I know that goal was not what I was there to accomplish.

I spent the next six weeks very intently studying the new teaching philosophies as well as trying desperately to soak up any horsemanship that I had not learned in my previous thirty weeks of courses. The greatest lesson I learned was how futile it is to compare my journey with anyone else's. There were several people both in the course as well as teaching the course that I felt hadn't paid the dues that I had and that they must have just happened to be in the right place at the right time. I found their good fortune and success infuriating! There was an instructor there that didn't "officially" have his level three at the beginning of the course, and he had never taken a University course, but somehow I was supposed to learn from him. There was a woman there that had her level three, but seemed so direct line to me. She never cut her horse any slack or gave him any affection. He seemed to always have to sing for his supper. She was always making him do tricks, even to earn a meal. It made me feel sorry for him. Then, to top it all off, a fellow student got her level 3 during this course. She had gotten to use a ranch lease horse to get this done, and it seemed like cheating to me. I tortured myself feeling as though I was being singled out and purposely held back. I was trying so hard. Why didn't they want me? It would take me several more years to come to accept that my journey has nothing to do with anyone else's and that comparing myself to anyone but what I consider to be the best version of me would result only in pain. And that pain was self inflicted. I could control it by learning to control my focus. What things mean to me, is up to me. I also learned that the more I could celebrate others' success, the more I would attract success to myself.

I would complete that course still without my level three. So, the total came to thirty-six weeks of courses, thousands of dollars, and countless moments in the lives of loved ones that I would never get back. I had missed Thanksgiving, birthdays, anniversaries, my oldest step-daughter's graduation, and the death of my grandmother. I felt pain. I felt despair. I felt as though I had let my husband and my family down. I was not accustomed to not achieving the goals that I set out to accomplish. I came very close to giving up at that point. Fortunately, my husband new that I would regret that decision. He knew that giving up would cause me to return to the unhappy person I had been prior to my Parelli experiences. And everyone knows that if momma ain't happy, ain't nobody happy. We had run out of resources for paying for another course. So my husband suggested that I could stay immersed in the horsemanship if I could convince the Parelli organization to give me a job. I will always be grateful for Shane's wisdom, generosity and love.

Touring With Parelli

In June of 2006, I begged the Parelli organization for a job and due to my resilience and experience, I was invited to join the tour team. This was a team of folks who traveled all over the country to help spread the message of Parelli Natural Horsemanship. Linda and Pat Parelli travel all over the world putting on seminars to educate the public about the Parelli program and how to understand what it is our horses are trying to tell us. They give people hope and empower them to live their dreams. I was very excited to become a member of this team. Finally, I felt a sense of acceptance and belonging within the Parelli organization. Little did I know that the universe had some very important lessons for me to learn during this time. All of my dedication and hard work was going to pay off.

The tour team lived a fairly extreme lifestyle. We all lived in travel trailers together and worked ten to fourteen hour days together as well. We lived and worked in very close quarters and there was little room for privacy or to be an individual. It was imperative that we work as a team. And the best advice I got was on my first day. My leader said to me, "Try to not piss anyone off." I remember at the time feeling as though that was pretty weird advice. It would not take long for me to understand what he meant. We had a job to do and there was no room for personal conflicts to get in the way of that job. There was a team of four women, including me, that all lived in one travel trailer. For each seminar we would travel with the other vehicles required to put these events on. So, not only did we spend hours together at work, and at home, but we also spent days on end in trucks together crisscrossing the country. These days spent in-between seminars were very difficult for me. I was much older than the other girls. I was the only one that was married, and we were all very independent and strong willed. I have to say, there were actually very few blow outs amongst us. I believe the reason for that was the incredible experiences we got to have at each tour stop.

These seminars with Pat and Linda are a bit like a religious revival. People make realizations about not just horsemanship, but about life. There would be laughter and tears. I would often take moments to just step back and allow my gratitude for the experiences I was receiving to just wash over me. I was for sure increasing my horsemanship, but more than that I was increasing my appreciation for the human spirit. Every seminar would bring an overwhelming sense of gratitude and excitement for what was possible. I grew up feeling that people could live better than what I was experiencing if they could just learn to choose better. Here it was! People would open their minds and listen to what Linda and Pat had to say with an open heart and a deep appreciation for the horse and the people who want to make the world a better place.

Remember Me Well

I didn't get to spend much time with my horse Maxi that summer. We were on the road quite a bit. Even when we were at home base in Pagosa Springs, I spent a great deal of time in the office. So as we started to make plans to make the move to the Florida campus that fall, I decided that I wasn't going to take my horse with me. The days were getting shorter because the summer was ending and I just did not feel it would serve her or me for her to make that long trip. I began to make arrangements for her to go home to Iowa. Luckily, there was a student at the center that lived within 4 hours of my house and who agreed to take her as far as his home in Kansas. My husband agreed to pick her up there.

This was in the late summer of 2006. My life had been centered on my time with my horse for nearly two years at this point. Needless to say, I was feeling pretty emotional about sending her home. Total immersion in Parelli twenty-four hours a day seven days a week can be a pretty intense experience. Maxi was my buddy who I turned to when I needed a friend and some down time. As I prepared to send her home, I came to realize that I was really going to miss her. The thought of it was breaking my heart.

A few days before her departure, I went to play with her. And, for the first time, I considered what she would be thinking at the end of that session. Not because some instructor had told me that I should, but because I really wanted to leave her with happy thoughts of me. She had plenty of reason to have unpleasant thoughts. Lucky for me, she lives in the moment and forgives me when I do better. It was the first time I went to her and said, what do you want to do today, and really meant it. It was amazing what showed up that day—flying lead changes! I had been trying to force them for the last eighteen months. And the moment I said to her, "Today, your needs are my needs," she offered flying lead changes.

You see, I was living with a good little predator paradigm, or an attitude of scarcity. What does a dog do with a bone? He buries it in case there isn't another one coming and so that another dog can't get it. Our culture would have us believe that there is some proverbial pie out there and we are each slotted a certain piece. If you get a bigger piece, it is because you took some of mine. Or if I stop fighting to get my needs met, then they never will be met. I will do without.

The moment I cared more about my horse's needs than my outcomes, my outcomes came fairly regularly. Maxi was teaching me how to put our relationship ahead of my goals and she continues to do so today. Her opinion of me is more important than any behavior I can solicit. I want to be able to put my arm over her neck at the end of a session and say, "Was it as good for you as it was for me?" and have her be able to say yes. I challenge you to ask not what your partner can do for you today, but what you can do for your partner. You might just be surprised at how often your needs get met. If I can improve the quality of her life, she just might improve the quality of mine. Imagine how that attitude could enhance every relationship in our lives. What if we could focus on improving the quality of each other's lives based on our partners needs and not our own? What would be possible if we could say to one another,

"Nothing is more important to me than your needs."? What if we could trust and be brave enough to be vulnerable? What if we didn't cling so desperately to what we need, but instead started to focus on what we can give. What if? I think that the "Golden Rule" should be reworded. I think it should be, "Do un to others as they would have done to them."

CHAPTER 6

Level Three

IN NOVEMBER OF 2006, all of my blood, sweat, and tears finally seemed to have been worth it. While I was on tour with Pat and Linda, I finally achieved my level three! When you achieve a new level of horsemanship in the Parelli program, you are awarded a horseman's string that signifies the level of horsemanship or as Pat would say savvy, that you have accomplished to all who study the program. It is similar to the belt colors for karate. The level 1 award is a red string. The level two award is a blue string. The level three string is green. And the level 4 string is black. I had spent thirty-six weeks of courses, 6 months on tour, and countless hours of independent study torturing my poor horse trying to accomplish all of the tasks on the level three lists. Finally, my day had come! And the best part was that Pat awarded me my string in front of a crowd of about 2,000 people at a tour stop in Tennessee. It was one of the greatest moments of my career. Mr. Parelli was singling me out in front of a crowd and acknowledging all of my hard work and achievements. I felt validated and appreciated. It was amazing! Pat tied the sting around my neck in what is called a celebration knot. It made me feel very special. As a member of the Parelli clan, I very diligently carry a horseman's string in my back pocket. I couldn't wait for that string to be green. But, I was not going to put that string in my pocket. Pat himself had tied it around my neck. I wore it around my neck for days. Finally, I ended up conning an instructor into giving me another one so that I could keep my special knotted one knotted. It is still knotted and hanging on display in my office.

Faculty Invitation

A few weeks after achieving level three and receiving my green string from Pat, I got some more good news. I was on the road with the tour team in Louisville, Kentucky. We were in Kentucky promoting the Parelli program at the national arabian horse show there. It is a week-long horse show and we had been there for several days. At the end of a long day, I was back at our travel trailer checking my emails from the day. I came to one that was from one of my Parelli mentors. I couldn't imagine what she might be emailing me about. It was a very short and very important email for me. Really there was only one sentence. "Would you be interested in joining the faculty?"

The faculty was a team of people handpicked to teach the Parelli program at the Parelli centers. I had only just received my level three a few weeks earlier and already I was getting invited to teach! I was so excited! This is what I had been working for. The opportunity to teach at the centers full time was mind blowing. After I read the email, I started jumping up and down and squealing like a little girl. I didn't fully understand at the time what I was being invited to do. But I knew that I wanted to be a part of this program in the worst way and, I was excited to find out what being on Faculty would mean.

I would later find out that being on Faculty meant committing to three years of full-time employment at the Parelli Centers in

Colorado and Florida. That meant three years away from home, three years of missed birthday parties, family gatherings, vacations, and weekend neighborhood gatherings. On the other side, it was a chance of a lifetime. This would be an opportunity to learn to be a Parelli Instructor at the centers with the support of Pat and Linda personally. I would have the support of a team, access to the amazing centers, and opportunities to travel the world. I knew that I wanted to at least give it a try.

My husband and I had many long talks about what we should do. It was pretty scary and painful to think about being away from each other for such a long time. I had experienced some intense homesickness while I was taking courses and on tour. This commitment would ensure that I would go through that pain for another three years. That alone made it difficult for me to commit. On the other hand, Shane and I had run out of resources to pay for any more schooling. Even though I had achieved level three, I still needed more time in the University to gain certification as a Parelli Instructor. I could gain that certification on faculty and get paid while I was doing it. I knew that I would regret passing on this opportunity for the rest of my life. I had to at least try. Shane and I made one promise to each other. If at any time either of us began to feel as though my absence was going to cost us our marriage, we would rethink our decision and put our marriage first. I had no idea at the time how difficult that would be.

Living The Dream

I began my time on Faculty in January 2007. I had never experienced so many conflicting emotions at once. I was scared and excited. I was hopeful and self conscious. I was worried about who I would become if I left and who I would never become if I didn't. I was scared that I would fail. I was terrified that my marriage would fail. I had such terrible feedback in the university that I was concerned about not being ready for this challenge. What if I hadn't done enough personal growth? I felt a great deal of responsibility for the people I would be coaching. I was in debt up to my ears, and I felt a responsibility to my family to make this work. I didn't want to let anyone down. It was a pretty intense time in my life.

My first several weeks on the faculty team were spent doing a lot of fetch and carry sort of tasks. I was happy to have the time to just observe and take in what was to be expected of me. But it wasn't long before I was informed that I was expected to start *teaching*. Then, to increase my anxiety, I was expected to teach the piece of the Parelli program that I felt the least comfortable with. The subject is called finesse and it is the most advanced and intricate piece of the program. Finesse is the part of my level three that held me back for eighteen months. I have heard that you should teach that which you most need to learn. It was going to be a trial by fire. Luckily, I had a great team to lean on and learn from. I was given several weeks of notice before my first presentation and everything went fine. There were, of course, things that I needed to improve on, but I felt successful.

The next challenge I was going to have to face would be participating in a colt start course. A strong knowledge of what it takes to put the first ten to twenty rides on a horse that has never been ridden before is a very valuable skill set for any horsemanship instructor to have. It was a great privilege and an extremely valuable opportunity for me to have. There were only two problems with that opportunity. First, I was terrified of colt starting due to my experiences in college and the few years after. Secondly, my time on the tour team had a very noticeable side effect. I had gained about thirty pounds. To be effective at starting colts, one must be athletic and fit. I couldn't do much about being scared, but I sure as heck was not going to be the fat kid in the class.

I had a few months to prepare myself mentally and physically. And since I didn't feel as though I could do much about my fear, I began to focus on my body. I began jogging everyday and really making better decisions about what I ate. I had tried to get back in shape while I was on tour, but I just couldn't muster the self discipline. But the thought of being physically unable to perform the tasks required for colt starting in front of my peers was enough to get me up early and keep me up late. The pain of that possible outcome was more motivating than the pleasure I could get from eating. Unfortunately, it only worked until the colt start. I am very proud to say that I was in better shape by the time the colt start came around and physically I was ready.

Mentally, I was a wreck. I had had such terrible experiences in this area of study, and I really did not want to do it. The only reason I did was because I wanted to be the best instructor I could possibly be. I knew that I needed this experience to get there. Everything went really well. The horse that I was assigned did great. He was a nice little confident chestnut quarter horse. I later learned that he had a history of pulling back, but I never experienced that with him. I was originally assigned a horse that ended up bolting on the first day that we rode, and the person assigned to that horse got pretty banged up. The instructor ended up having to ride the horse and help him over the initial shock of accepting a rider. I was so relieved that I was not the one to be on board when that horse freaked out. I had a good experience. But I must admit that I do not really think that I learned very much in that colt starting course. I was just too nervous to remember much of what we were meant to learn. It would not be until the next colt start course that I would really learn something about colt starting horsemanship and how I could improve my skill set.

I did begin to understand one very important aspect of becoming a horseman during that course. On the first day, our instructor took us out to a grassy hill and lined us all up. He asked for our trust and faith in him to guide us through the process. Little did he know at the time what a tall order he was asking me for. It was a gorgeous sunny morning and we were staring at the San Juan Mountains that surround the Parelli Colorado campus. It was a very surreal moment. In addition to our faith, our instructor asked us to leave our ego on the hill upon which we were standing. He told us that we could come get it there at the end of this three-week course if we wanted to, but for the duration of the course we should leave it there. This was a very important exercise for me. Trust and ego are two things that are very difficult for me. The last time I had trusted someone to counsel me during a colt starting process, I had ended up in the emergency room discussing the possibility of internal bleeding. I was also still clinging very tightly to my ego. The thought of being put in any sort of compromising situation made me extremely uncomfortable. My anxiety about the course grew.

During the next few weeks, I would be presented with many opportunities to see where my limitations were. A great example of that would be the sessions in which we would ride something referred to as the extreme seat builder. This is a tool used to help us learn how to ride a bucking colt. The idea is to have it be in a controlled situation so that you can get some coaching and increase your skill set. My ego and lack of faith prevented me from really benefitting from these sessions. I was so uncomfortable being put in such a compromising situation that all I could do was resist the instruction that I was being given. There is a term in horse training called "turning loose." This happens when a horse decides with certainty that you are his or her friend and would never do anything to harm them and decides to willingly and happily accept your leadership. That is what I needed to do in those sessions in order to learn from them. I couldn't. All I managed to do is survive. At the end of the course I was relieved, but also disappointed that I was still bound by the fears that I had gained in college. I did not realize at the time how hard I was going to have to work and how long it would take to rebuild my confidence.

My next opportunity to participate in a colt starting course would be six months later. This course would have a very different outcome. This course was at the Florida Parelli campus. We had the same instructor and the course ran pretty similarly to the first one I had attended. In these courses, we would begin each day by circling the colts in an exercise called a rodear. Once we had the colts in the center of our circle, then each participant would present themselves to the mob of colts and allow the one that was drawn to them to choose them for the day. This exercise allowed us to get to play with several of the young horses on the ground. There were lots of exercises that the colts needed to understand before we would start to consider riding them. During these days, we were encouraged to notice the whole herd and to keep our perspective broad and not get overly focused on just the horse we were playing with in the moment. As a group we had all picked out a young black filly as one of the most difficult in the herd. She was the type of horse who seemed to just be tolerating the humans and not really turning loose to anything or anyone. She would freeze up and sometimes even fall over when anyone put too much pressure on her. This is the type of horse who is prone to exploding when she feels over-faced.

Because of my previous colt starting experience in Colorado, I was feeling some confidence, and I secretly hoped that I would get to be the one to put the first ride on the little black introverted filly. She was just the sweetest little thing, and I felt as though I could take things slow enough for her and keep her confidence intact. I really wanted to give it a try anyway. As I think back on it now, I just wanted the glory of being able to say that I was the one to ride her. I was coming from my ego and that little filly took it upon herself to let me know that fact. I did get chosen to ride her first, but things did not go as I planned.

The first time that we rode these young horses was in a large round corral with about seven or eight colts at a time in a group. Keeping them in a herd like that helped each horse to maintain their confidence and the instructor could move us about with his saddle horse. We were not meant to do much other than stay out of the horses' way. Essentially we were passengers. The instructor was controlling everyone's horses with a flag. This ride went really well. The little black filly granted me a walk, trot, and canter with very little bobbles. She did great and I was bursting with pride. I thought that would be the hardest part and that the next ride would be fine. I relaxed too much and would soon find out how arrogant that was.

The next day we rode the entire mob together in an arena. It was a beautiful, sunny, but brisk morning in Florida. I remember being a little concerned that my little black filly would get a fright from my jacket. It was kind of baggy and made a swishy noise when I moved my arms. She did not react to that at all.

There were around twenty other young horses with us that day. And everything went really well while we were in the arena. We all walked, trotted and cantered as a group. We turned left and right. It was time for these young horses' first ride out, meaning ride outside of an arena. When it comes to colt starting, it is important to stay progressive. This keeps the young horse just stimulated enough to stay in the conversation, but hopefully not so stimulated that they feel overwhelmed. Our instructor opened the gait to the arena and as a group we headed out into the wide open spaces. My heart was racing, but all I could think of was how special *I* was to be riding this little filly.

Our instructor took us through another gate. We were going to use a hill to ask the herd for their first canter. Cantering a young horse uphill helps them to learn how to balance a rider's weight at this gait. As I passed through the gate, I looked over at our instructor. He gave me a wink and I took that as a compliment on how well I was doing. I held my little filly back and let the rest of the herd go by before following them up the hill. I had noticed in previous sessions that she did not feel comfortable out front. Whenever she happened to end up there, she would hunker down and make her way to the back of the herd all the while getting kicked and bitten. Being in a "me" state of mind, I did not want to be on her while she was getting kicked and bitten. I thought I was doing the right thing, but I was doing the right thing for me and not for her. The truth was, I was scared to death to be out front. But, that would have been the best place for the filly. Out front, she would have needed to rely on my leadership. When I held her back and let her follow the herd, she started to rely on the herd's leadership. Once she transferred the leadership to the herd she kind of fell asleep in motion. She pretty much lost all track of me. Then when I leaned back and asked her for a canter she woke up and was not happy to find me on top of her. She began to buck and my mind went blank. I could not recall any of the advice given to me on the extreme seat builder and therefore was promptly ejected. Luckily, I was not hurt physically, the only things injured that day were my pride and my confidence.

I had to walk up the hill to retrieve my horse, fighting back tears the whole way. Not because I was hurt, but because I was embarrassed and frustrated. I had been such a jackass all week, bragging about how the instructor had chosen me for this filly. I knew that I had let her down, but I wanted someone else to blame. My instructor had taken the filly and helped her to calm down again. He asked me if I was okay and if I wanted to get back on her. My pride was not going to let me say no. Inside I was screaming *NO!* But, I got back on her anyway. About twenty minutes later, I was eating dirt again. It was humiliating. But, as I think about it now, I realize that I really let that little filly down. She entrusted me with the privilege of being the first human to ride her, and I let her down. It is very important time in a young horse's life, and I had let that one down. I got focused on myself and my own needs. And, because of that, that little filly had a pretty unfair start to her riding career.

Losing Me

A lot of folks dream of becoming a Parelli instructor because they fall in love with the empowerment they feel when they start to understand the program and they love horses, so they think, why not teach it. But, to teach the Parelli program, you must also be fascinated by people. I had a mentor tell me that in my first ten week course. I remember being taken back by that. At the time, I was not sure I was fascinated by people. I just loved horses, and I loved Parelli. So, I thought that is all I would need to be a Parelli instructor. I was wrong.

During my first weeks on the faculty team, I would grow my fascination of people. I was presented with information on basic personality types and how to recognize each one. I was given a set of DVDs created by Linda Parelli on how to identify each of those personality types as a means to be a better communicator. I couldn't help but try to analyze myself first. One day after work I had been watching the DVDs in my bedroom. I emerged to announce that I wasn't sure which one I was, but I was certain which one I wasn't. All it took was for one of my friends to say "oh really?" and I became uncertain again. I thought those two little words meant that she thought that I was that personality type. I trusted and respected her and her opinion was really important to me. She had more experience than me and so probably knew better than I did. Those two little words caused me to see myself through that filter for nearly six months. I worked very hard to be that personality. I convinced others that the core values of that personality were mine.

The personality type that I was trying to be is the type of person who holds their emotions on the inside and who wants to make sure that everyone they care about is okay. Six months later I was in a meeting with the faculty team and Linda Parelli. We were actually discussing a model on diagnosing a horse's "personality" using the model that we had learned about people. So we were sitting there discussing introverts and extroverts, left brain and right brain people. All the while, I was chewing gum. Now, when my feet are still and I have bubble gum in my mouth, I wouldn't exactly call what I do to it chewing. It is more like I attack it. It is pretty annoying, and I try not to have gum in my mouth in meetings, but I did in this one instance. So, we were sitting there talking to Linda and discussing our own personalities when Linda said to me, "Kristi, do you think you are an introvert or an extrovert?" And as I attacked my gum, I assured her that I was certain I was an introvert. She then asked me if my gum was good. I was immediately embarrassed because I know how annoying I can be with gum in my mouth. Linda then informed me that what I was doing was a displaced behavior and that introverts don't generally chew gum and if they did no one around them would know it.

I had worked so hard to be that introvert, but Linda's words were clear and believable. Of course I am extrovert! I already had folks tell me that they could see if I was having a good or bad day from a mile away. What was I thinking? What I learned from this was to be careful with my words. Even words that seem to be insignificant can significantly influence someone's path. My friend did not intend to steer me wrong. She was just having a conversation with me. But, her words had a profound impact. This awareness would paralyze me for months.

The next realization I would have about my personality would be much more painful. Each course we ran on the Parelli campuses would end with a finale that included a feedback form. The Parelli organization is very keen to encourage their instructors to be in a state of constant improvement and accountability. There was a reoccurring theme on the feedback forms in the courses that I was teaching. "Kristi is very knowledgeable, but it took me awhile to warm up to her." I had two reactions from a great majority of our students. Either they were really pissed at me, or I had them crying. I was really baffled by that early on. I was really trying to help people. But, somehow my approach was not coming across as help. I was making things worse.

My bold and direct approach to coaching was causing folks to feel as though I didn't care about them. I was too quick to give advice. I needed to spend more time getting to know my students and allowing them to get to know me. I thought they just wanted to have the information that had been shared with me. It turned out that they wanted a relationship with me first.

I was about to embark on a very difficult path that I am still on today. I was learning all kinds of really great tools for sharing information in different ways depending on how a student needed to hear it. It just so happens that a great majority of our student body happen to be my opposite. That does not mean right or wrong, it just means that we have different learning and communicating strategies. However, as their instructor it is up to me to communicate with them in a way that they find palatable. Doing this caused me to lose track of myself for a very long time. I spent so much time trying to be who everyone needed me to be that I lost track of myself. To be honest I am still struggling with that one. But, I know that not all personal revelations happen in one magical moment. Some need to brew for awhile before the lesson can be learned.

Relax and Enjoy the Journey

One of the things that got me really interested in the Parelli program was seeing folks ask their horses to lie down. I thought, "Boy, if I could get a horse to do that, I bet I could get them to do about anything." So, along with achieving strings and instructor certification, I was also now obsessed with asking my horse to lie down. I had asked several instructors about how to go about teaching that. The only response I could get was when you are ready to ask for it, you will know how to. I really did *not* like that answer.

I have heard Pat say that one of his mentors told him that his greatest asset was his ambition. They also said his greatest fault was his ambition. If you have been involved in the Parelli program very long, and you are the ambitious sort, you have probably heard someone say just relax and enjoy the journey. Ahhhh!!! Boy, did I hate it when someone would tell me that. I will relax and enjoy the journey when you give me the dang string and stars! I was so focused on my desired outcome that I couldn't appreciate the value of what I was going through.

Prior to me running off and joining the circus, which is how I often describe my Parelli journey, I had asked for advice from several of the top-ranking instructors. My question was, "How can I get the most out of this experience?" I was getting ready to borrow a *bunch* of money to finance my education, and I wanted to do everything that I could to ensure that I achieved my desired outcomes, which was levels strings and instructor stars. The best advice I got was from five star senior instructor David Ellis. He said that I should borrow enough money that it didn't matter how long it took me to get there. *What!?!?* At the time, I thought it was the most ridiculous thing anyone had ever said to me. It wasn't until after I achieved level 3 that I realized how wise that advice was, no matter how unrealistic.

I have had several opportunities to learn to appreciate the journey, but none so much as learning to teach my horse to lay down. Pat has taught us that asking your horse to lie down is one of the most difficult things to ask your horse to do. I had seen this process done, and even done it myself where the horse didn't really have much choice. It is one of the things that I regret the most about my pre-Parelli journey. However, I made a promise to my horse Maxi that I would never do more than suggest that she lay down. If it took more than that to get her to do it, then it wasn't worth it.

The first time that Maxi lay down in my presence was in 2004 at a level two clinic in Iowa City, IA. She was just two years old at the time and it was an incredible experience for me. The class was standing around reflecting on something we had just learned. My feet were tired, so I knelt down to rest. A moment after I knelt down,

Maxi laid down next to me to rest too. I was blown away! It was the greatest feeling! I really wanted her to do it again!

The next time the lie down showed up would be 6 months later at my first Parelli course in Florida. I was spending undemanding time with Maxi in her pen and she laid down. She even went so far as to place her head in my lap! Oh my goodness, I just melted. I cried like a baby. I had such reverence for what it means for a prey animal to do that, I just completely lost it.

It would be five years later that she would willingly lie down because I asked her to. I set up a program of baths and sand nearly every day for the three years that I was on the Parelli faculty team. I think of that journey every time I feel as though I have been ineffective or misunderstood in any relationship. The relationships that I find the most challenging are the ones that I have with my step-daughters. These two young women are the most incredible people that I know. And, I want so badly to protect them from mistakes and pain. But Maxi has helped me to realize that all I can do is make a suggestion, and then allow them to respond however they choose. I have to just relax and enjoy the journey, even when it seems to not go the way that I would like for it to. I believe that it is okay for me to have a destination in mind, but it is up to my partners on that trip to decide on the route that will get us there. My goal is always to achieve a space that has everyone feeling empowered and successful. But I cannot control what it will take to get there. Everything happens for a reason, and if you are open to it, all experiences can help us to grow and bring us closer together. You cannot hurry these things. I am still learning to relax and enjoy the journey.

My path to becoming a Parelli instructor has been an intense journey of complete accountability and learning to take charge of the results I get. I have learned to understand how my innate characteristics affect other people and to strategize ways to present myself that allows others to find it easier to accept the information they are asking me for as their horsemanship instructor. Before I started this journey, I was completely unaware of how I affected people. I had no idea that what I considered confidence and determination, others were seeing as rigid and bullish. I knew that sometimes I could not get my information out because of the way I was presenting myself, but I did not posses the skills and habits to do anything differently. I was so excited to begin learning ways to adapt my approach that would empower me to get a different result.

Somewhere in those years of learning how to become a better horseman and instructor I developed a belief that being myself was not going to allow me to reach my goals. I began to believe that my innate characteristics were undesirable and that if I wanted to succeed in my dream career with people and horses, I was going to have to become someone else. I even had a mentor tell me that perhaps I should consider that I had chosen the wrong path. I seemed to be a round peg trying to shove myself into a square hole.

Over the last six years I have truly embraced the path of never ending self improvement, sometimes to the point of obsession. This obsession has served me well. I am thankful for all that I have learned about people and adjusting my approach to fit what is needed by the student in front of me, just as I would adjust my approach to help a horse at the end of the rope depending on their needs as an individual. What I lost along the way was an appreciation and love for myself.

For me, this journey has been about relationships and learning that I can take charge of my world and the relationships that support the type of reality that I would like to live in. The relationship that has suffered is the one that I have with myself. I have recently come to appreciate the limitations that I have put on myself by not honoring and loving my true and whole self. Not just the parts that are easy to be proud of, but the parts that are ugly and dark. I want my horse to believe that I love all of her, and that I want to help bring out her natural talents. I cannot do that without appreciating her limitations and loving her because of them, not in spite of them. I am determined to practice that unconditional love for myself so I develop it as a habit that will be easy to apply to my horsemanship and all relationships in my life.

From the Corn Fields of the Midwest to the Desert Sands of the Middle East

When I joined the faculty team, I really hoped that I was going to get opportunities to travel. Never in my wildest dreams did I imagine that those travels would take me to the Middle East. Be careful what you wish for. It was the most amazing experience!

From the moment I stepped off the plane at the Dubai International airport, I was out of my comfort zone. The environment was so surreal and a bit scary at first. This was the first time I had traveled anywhere that English wasn't the native language. I started to imagine how horses must feel when they get frightened and don't know how to ask for help. *What if I can't find my people?*, I thought to myself. How will I get help? My growing fear caused me to be acutely aware of my surroundings. No one around me seemed friendly and I started to feel extremely claustrophobic. Potential dangers lurked around every corner and I felt undeniably alone.

I made my way to the loading and unloading area, but I saw no evidence of the people who were meant to pick me up. I was surrounded by strangers who did not speak my language. I felt transparently vulnerable. I had to wait in that environment for twenty minutes before my ride showed up. During that time I created all kinds of possible scenarios in my mind. With each mental scenario I created either a plan of attack or defense. Talk about getting into my horse's skin! The danger I fabricated was all in my head, but it didn't matter, I was a prey animal in survival mode.

Finally, I heard my name being shouted and I turn to see smiling faces. Just their friendly expressions made all the difference and the tension that had been building started to subside. *I found my herd!* I was no longer alone. I now know first hand what my horse is feeling when we get home from a long trip and she rushes to be with her herd. It was such a relief to finally have someone there to show me what to do next.

The first few days I was in Dubai are a bit of a blur. There wasn't much time for lots of getting to know one another as I needed to be ready to slide into my new role within a couple of days. I was there to teach natural horsemanship for a company called HoofbeatZ. HoofbeatZ is a company that offers many different types of opportunities for the general public to enjoy horses. One way was to offer horsemanship lessons. They were getting ready to send their natural horsemanship instructor to the U.S. to study at the Florida Parelli center and I would be helping out in her absence. I needed to get familiar with her responsibilities as soon as possible.

I had three duties to look after. I was there to facilitate the continued education of the HoofbeatZ staff that included grooms, professional trainers, and office staff. I was also there to train a few horses, primarily four very special Arabians. Finally, I would teach a few private and group lessons for the general public. Little did I know, that these three things were going to draw on every bit of experience I had and some that I didn't.

To begin with, the range of experience within the HoofbeatZ staff was broad. I had people who were world renowned for their skills as horse trainers, on down to folks who had never laid a hand on a horse before. One moment I might be teaching someone who had experience with upper level competition maneuvers and then a few hours later I would be explaining where the withers are on a horse. I really learned to not make any assumptions about what a person might now about horses.

My time with the general public was the most difficult. These folks do not have easy access to the Parelli home study programs. I came to really appreciate how valuable this support network is to our students. These people's only knowledge of the Parelli program had come second hand. Most of them had never seen Pat and Linda, not even in a video. It was amazing to me that somehow they were still inspired enough to come and spend some time with me. Watching Pat and Linda is usually what inspires people to want to study the Parelli program. The people that we teach at the Parelli centers are the most dedicated Parelli students out there. They turn their lives upside down to learn from us. I had no idea what it would be like to try and help people who weren't already actively studying the program.

The horses that I had been assigned to train were a great source of satisfaction and comfort. They were Arabian horses and they awoke in me a love for the breed. Each one came with a history of neglect and/or abuse. HoofbeatZ and their director Eileen Verdieck have a vision of rehabilitating retired or cast away horses and giving them a new lease on life and a second chance at happiness. I felt a great sense of responsibility for these equines. I knew that their experience with humans had not always been great and I felt a compelling desire to improve their opinion of my species. They were ready to forgive. Being their partner for 6 weeks was my extreme privilege.

The work day began at about 6:30 in the morning. I would arrive at the stables to prepare for my morning sessions with the grooms. These sessions were the highlight of my days. The men on this team had no preconceived notions as to what I was there to teach them. They willingly and enthusiastically accepted the information I was there to give them. They were already doing some pretty amazing stuff by the time I got there. However, they were just going through the motions and not really reading their horses. With the help of a translator I was able to share with them how to interpret their horse's behavior and respond appropriately. Once I started giving them some basic patterns that allowed them to make their own decisions, their progress grew by leaps and bounds. This was a very talented and special group of men. I am a better person for having gotten to know them.

In the afternoons I would sometimes get to spend some time with the horse trainers that were there to create and develop the horse shows that Hoofbeatz put on. I really had to think about how I could inspire these folks to want to know more about Parelli. This was a very experienced group and they had a job to do that needed to happen on a specific timeline. In the Parelli program the horse is in charge of how long it takes to learn something new. This was not reality for these horses or humans. They had a show to produce and a deadline to meet. Here is where it could have been really easy for me to be righteous about my Parelli principles, and just be right at the wrong time. Instead, what I did was offer them information that could give them the results in the beginning and then little by little open their eyes to the relationship aspects. All of the people on this team were so wonderful to work with. I learned a lot from my time with them and I hope to get to see them again someday. I learned just as much from them as I could have ever hoped to teach.

Although I was out of my comfort zone for the entire six weeks, I will always remember my time in Dubai fondly. This experience really gave me some insight into just how difficult what Pat and Linda do for the Parelli brand really is. Pat always says that his job is inspiration and information, our job is dedication and perspiration. It is only when you get the first two right that the rest follows.

CHAPTER 7

What It All Means To Me

I GET THE sense that most people walk through life mostly unconscious. We wake up each day setting our sights on survival. If we end the day still on the top side of the grass, then we consider ourselves successful. We get caught up in the current of current affairs, current circumstances, current social events. We allow the flow of our current conditions to sweep us up and take us for a ride that we are not choosing for ourselves. Then we wonder to ourselves, *How did I get here?* We allow ourselves to be victimized by our circumstances. We place blame on others because it relieves us of the weight of the responsibility that comes with feeling in charge of our own destiny.

My horsemanship journey has taught me that I am creating my reality with every thought and every emotion. Pat Parelli teaches us that one of the greatest qualities a horseman can possess is the ability to control our focus and that we should be careful with our thoughts. I do not live in your reality. I live in a reality that is only real for me. What that means to me is that I am making it up. So, if I am making it up, then I may as well make it something good.

Maxi helped me to realize that(along with Linda Parelli's help) when we were trying to advance our relationship at Liberty or without any ropes attached to her. I was teaching on the Parelli Faculty team in Reddick, FL. We were learning how to create more dynamic demonstrations with several different professionals, including dancers from Juliard and the head dolphin trainer at Discovery Cove, Lynn Eisenhardt. We were all meant to pick a song and create an "MTV music video". We were to think about what kind of a feeling we wanted to create in our audience and put some choreography to music. We were learning to be better showman.

Maxi had other lessons to teach me at this time. She did not care that I was trying to convey an emotion and stick to some choreography that went with the song. I was getting too direct line with my thinking and she was trying to tell me that by leaving me every time I tried to do one of the tricks that I had planned for my performance.

Lucky for me, Linda was having a similar problem with one of her horses around this same time. One of the greatest gifts I received while on the Parelli Faculty team was getting to spend time with Linda Parelli. During one of our sessions with her, she described to us what was going on with her horse and a revelation that she had come to. Instead of thinking that her horse "left" her, she considered that he had merely taken the leadership. And, instead of challenging him for it, she gave it to him and became a follower in that moment. What that looks like is she would ask him to do something and he would mentally disconnect and physically run away from her. Instead of trying to get him to come back to her, she would follow him. This was all happening in a 50' round corral. Her horse was leaving out of fear and when she followed him instead of putting pressure on him to come back to her, his confidence grew.

Maxi didn't often choose to leave me out of fear. She was leaving out of dominance and a dislike for the conversation I was trying to have with her. However, the same strategy worked for her that worked for Linda and her horse. Instead of getting into an argument with her about who was leading who, I simply gave the leadership to her. And then, little by little when she was ready, she would give it back to me. My thought for her was, *You can go if you want to, but you are not getting rid of me.* We soon got to a point where we were swapping the leadership moment to moment and the results were magical.

Initially I was feeling victimized by my horse. *How could she do this to me?,* I had thought. Even as I write that now, I am embarrassed that I could have such a thought. It wasn't until I could think to myself, *What is she trying to tell me?,* that I was able to change the results I was getting. It is interesting because at the time I thought I was controlling my focus by not allowing the environment to shift my thoughts. When I was rehearsing this performance, there were often people around watching. I felt so proud of myself for being able to tune them out and be in the moment with my horse. But, I was still not in control of my thoughts. I was allowing my horse's response to my suggestions to dictate how I felt about myself and the situation. I had handed over my personal power to my horse. How ridiculous! The only thing I had to change was the meaning that I was giving to those responses and my whole experience changed to a positive and progressive one. I changed the meaning by changing my focus and thoughts. Instead of thinking, *Why are you doing this to me?,* I thought, *What can I do better for you?* And that made all of the difference in the world.

Final Thoughts

The quality of my life can be measured by the quality of my relationships and the mastery I am looking for is mastery of myself. My life is created by my thoughts and I can control my thoughts and focus. The horses in my life have taught me many things. Perfection is unrealistic, but mastery of oneself is exquisite. There are always at least 2 ways to interpret any situation and that my version is only real to me. My needs get met when my partners needs are my needs. I can only become a victim if I hand over my personal power. I am capable of more than just what mother-nature has equipped me with for survival. I cannot offer advice and have it mean anything unless I have been asked for it. If I am looking for a way to be heard, I should begin by listening with an intention to gain a heartfelt understanding. And the greatest lesson that my horses have taught me is that if I keep my mind and heart focused on love, all that I desire is already mine.

CPSIA information can be obtained at www.ICGtesting.com
Printed in the USA
LVOW041412240412

278939LV00008B/122/P